CASE STUDIES IN
CULTURAL ANTHROPOLOGY

GENERAL EDITORS

George and Louise Spindler

STANFORD UNIVERSITY

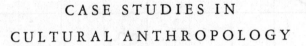

THE TIWI OF NORTH AUSTRALIA

THE TIWI OF NORTH AUSTRALIA

BY

C. W. M. HART
University of Wisconsin

AND

ARNOLD R. PILLING
Wayne State University

HOLT, RINEHART AND WINSTON NEW YORK

March, 1962
Copyright © 1960
by Holt, Rinehart and Winston, Inc.
Library of Congress Catalog Card Number: 60-7332

23487-0110

Printed in the United States of America

About the Authors

C. W. M. HART was born in Australia and became an American citizen in 1953. He studied at the Universities of Sydney, Chicago, and London; and has taught anthropology at the London School of Economics, University of Toronto, and the University of Wisconsin where he is now professor of anthropology. He was associate editor of the *American Anthropologist* from 1949 to 1952 and was recently elected president of the Society for Applied Anthropology.

Arnold R. Pilling, a Californian, studied at the University of California at Berkeley. He was a Fulbright Fellow to Australia in 1953 and 1954 and spent most of that time studying the culture of the Tiwi. He is now a member of the Department of Sociology and Anthropology at Wayne State University in Detroit.

About the Book

This is a case study of a system of influence and power which is based on a strange currency. The currency is woman. Newborn females, nubile marriageable females, toothless old hags — all are valuable in Tiwi terms. Because men compete for prestige and influence through their control over women, women have the value of a scarce commodity. Under this system there are no illegitimate children, no unmarried females of any age, and wives are either very much older or very much younger than their husbands.

A vivid picture of Tiwi life, as viewed from within the culture, emerges in this book. The reader is not made an outsider, left to peer into a dimly understood, formalized, alien way of life. Rather, he is taken inside the family group, by the night's campfire. He becomes a witness to angry quarrels, a participant in involved machinations aimed at success — as defined by the Tiwi. He comes to know individual Tiwi as real people.

This book is a study of social interaction. But it is also a study of culture change. Much happened between Hart's and Pilling's visits to the Tiwi. These changes are described, and we see them in the context of the period of Tiwi contacts with the outside world.

GEORGE AND LOUISE SPINDLER
General Editors

Stanford, California
December 1959

Preface

HART WORKED among the Tiwi during 1928 and 1929, and in Chapters 1, 2, 3, and 4 summarizes the main aspects of their culture as it was at that time. Pilling's fieldwork was carried out during 1953 and 1954, and he outlines in Chapter 5 the contacts of the Tiwi with the outside world before and up until the coming of the first missionaries in 1911, and in Chapter 6 describes the modifications in Tiwi culture that have occurred since 1930. It is rare for two anthropologists who have studied the same tribe at widely separated times to collaborate in writing about them, hence it is worth mention (1) that the two anthropologists had never met nor even written to each other until after Pilling had returned to the United States in 1955; (2) that when they finally got together during 1957-1958 to plan and write the present book, they were both astonished at how little basic disagreement there was between them. Arguments about each other's statements have been numerous and prolonged, but almost invariably these concerned matters of detail or emphasis. The chief result of the collaboration has been the discovery, by each author, and exciting for both, of how well the other knows his Tiwi. This is uncommon enough in anthropology to be noteworthy. We are both grateful to the Tiwi for having brought us together and we are both impressed by the fact that the Tiwi who brought us together were the same complicated but delightful people, despite the twenty-five year interval in our respective sojourns among them.

C.W.M.H.
A.R.P.

Madison, Wisconsin
Detroit, Michigan
December 1959

Contents

Top to bottom: Timalarua, the canoe maker; Tiwi spears; mourning ceremony around graveposts.

LOCATION OF THE BANDS

CAPE KEITH

CAPE VAN DIEMAN

TURUPULA

MELVILLE

YEIMPI

WILRANGWILA

MANDIIMBULA

MUNUPULA

APSLEY STRAIT

MALAUILA

MINGWILA

RANGWILA

TIKLAUILA

CAPE FOURCROY

CAPE GAMBIER

SCALE

10   20 MILES

WHITE LOCATIONS

1 FORT DUNDAS
2 GARDEN POINT
3 SNAKE BAY
4 R.C. MISSION
5 COOPERS HOUSE

Introduction:

The Australian Aborigines

The First Men in Australia

THOUGH EUROPEAN SEAFARERS, particularly the Portuguese and the Dutch, had sighted and even landed upon the shores of Australia at much earlier dates, the first real knowledge of Australia and what it contained was brought back to Europe by the great English explorer, Captain James Cook, as a result of his voyage of 1769-71. During that voyage, Cook surveyed and mapped most of the long eastern coastline of the island continent, and since he was a keen scientist himself and also had on board several naturalists, including the noted botanist Sir Joseph Banks, the wonders of the new country—its peculiar flora and fauna and its strange, primitive human inhabitants—were carefully examined and described for the first time. We may therefore fix the bringing of the Australian native peoples to the attention of the Western world as dating from Cook's discovery of 1770.

By that date, most of the rest of the world was known and at least some rough notions of what the existing races looked like were held by educated Europeans. Captain Cook and the naturalists with him were therefore quick to realize that the Australian natives, both in their physical appearance and way of life, were distinct from any people elsewhere. Dark skinned and wide nosed as they were, their low brows and wavy hair (including luxuriant beards) clearly differentiated them from the African Negroes, while the general crudity of their culture distinguished them from the dusky islanders of the Pacific. Physical type different from anybody else, culture simpler and more primitive—these were the two predominant impressions which the Australian natives made on the first Europeans to associate with them and they are still, to modern anthropologists, the two basic features that must be used when trying to place the Australians within the racial and cultural history of mankind.

Why the Australians—when finally discovered by the Europeans—should be so different in physical type and so primitive in culture compared with most of the world is usually explained by employing the same concept that

1

scientists use to account for the continued survival in Australia of eucalyptus trees, kangaroos, koala bears, and the duck-billed platypus—namely, the long-continued isolation of early forms, which elsewhere have either died out or changed into something a little more modern. Australia is a large and geologically an ancient country, but in relation to the other large land masses on the earth, it is very "cut-off" and remote. Recent white settlement in Australia has built up large modern cities which are similar in many respects to those in America. During World War II, American troops stationed in these Australian cities were astonished to find so many of their cherished American institutions —department stores, drug stores, movie theaters—located in a country "so far from everywhere." It is this isolation that accounts for the preservation in Australia of plants, animals, and a native race which, deprived of contact with the rest of the world until recently, developed or retained characteristics which are unique in the modern world.

Most of what we know about the first entry of men into Australia is based on probability and inference. Since Australia is in such an out-of-the-way corner of the earth's surface, man is not likely to have originated there. He must therefore have migrated—probably accidentally—from somewhere else. A glance at a world map will show that this migration can hardly have been from any continent other than Asia. The long chain of islands stretching down into the Pacific from the neighborhood of Singapore suggests the obvious migration route. There was a time in the geological past when many of these islands were joined to each other by land bridges which also tied them to Asia and Australia, so that early animals such as marsupials were able to walk (or hop) from Asia to Australia without getting their feet wet. But these land connections disappeared under the ocean long before the appearance of man on earth, and therefore the early ancestors of the Australians, in moving down from Asia through the islands, must have encountered stretches of open ocean on their route. Such inferences pose the general shape of the problem. The early Australians came from Southeast Asia; they came, part of the way at least, by water, and they must have remained isolated in Australia after their arrival.

How early in terms of years these first humans reached Australia can be inferred from indirect evidence. The crucial point is the simplicity of the Australians' tools and weapons. Present-day anthropology does not subscribe to the idea that human technological development has only been along a single line (the doctrine of unilineal cultural evolution), but nonetheless in a rough sense the presence or absence of certain basic pieces of human technology can be used as time indicators. When the Europeans first encountered the natives of southeastern Australia in the 1700's, the following items of technology were completely lacking among them: all use of metal, agriculture, domestic animals (except the dog), pottery, and the bow and arrow. As they had none of these in 1700, the belief is that their ancestors had none of them when they first arrived. Since those ancestors came from Asia via the islands, they must have left Asia before these items of culture were invented or known there. Agriculture, pottery, and metal using were developed comparatively late in human history, but the absence of knowledge of the bow and arrow in the southern parts of Australia is particularly notable since this weapon is relatively ancient and very wide-spread among hunting and gathering peoples. Moreover, its value to hunters is so great that it is unlikely to be given up. Hence, we infer that the earliest Australians migrated down from Southeast Asia at a time so early that knowledge of the bow and arrow had not yet reached that area. Evidence regarding the origin of the bow and arrow is still not certain. In Western Europe this weapon is usually dated as first appearing in the Mesolithic Period (roughly 20,000–6,000 B.C.). Dr. Kroeber includes the bow among the artifacts which the first ancestors of the American Indians carried across Bering Straits around 15,000 B.C. This last date will suffice as an approximation. By 15,000 B.C. the bow and arrow were present in Northeast Asia (that is, the section lying towards Bering Straits) and probably were also known in Southeast Asia. We may hazard the conclusion, therefore, that the ancestors of the Australians must have already left the vicinity of the Asiatic mainland by that date. This leads to the inference that when discovered by Captain Cook in 1770, the Australians had been in Australia for something like 17,000 years,[1] having drifted down from the mainland of Asia possessing only the primitive technological equipment that the rest of the world had evolved at that time. Having arrived "at the end of the line" in Australia, they could go no further, and survived there in isolation, keeping, but not improving upon, the simple technology they had brought with them.

But why were they left alone while other peoples, at later dates, with improved tools and weapons (including the bow and arrow) occupied the islands behind them and beyond them? For today the island chain from the mainland of Asia down to New Guinea and the numerous island groups further out into the Pacific (Melanesia, Micronesia, and Polynesia) are occupied by peoples who not only differ from the Australians in physical type but also possess such cultural items as the bow and arrow, agriculture, domesticated pigs, pottery, and many others, which were unknown in Australia. The answer to this second part of the problem seems to hinge upon the types of ocean transportation employed by these early migrants.

In reconstructing the early culture history of the Pacific region, it is impossible to operate without one general assumption—namely, that the type of tools (including the type of canoe) possessed by a given native people when the white man first arrived was approximately the same as that which the early ancestors of those people brought with them when they first entered the area in question. (This assumption can, of course, only be made if there is strong supporting evidence that changes in the tools (and canoes) *after arrival* were minimal or superficial.) On this assumption the early Australians

---

[1] So far, very little archaeological investigation has been carried out in Australia. The earliest dated cultural material from the continent is about 8,500 years old. However, Australian archaeologists have located human artifacts which apparently are earlier than this dated culture.

are thought to have arrived in the type of canoes that were still in use by their descendants in the 1700's. These craft, mostly in use in Cook's time on the northern and eastern coasts and the inland waterways, were called canoes by courtesy but were incredibly frail. They consisted of a single sheet of bark bent roughly into the shape of a boat, laced together at the ends, caulked with wild honeycomb or some vegetable gum, their sides held apart by a few sticks. Such "canoes" are little better than rafts; even in calm water they are likely to swamp, capsize, or disintegrate, and the only thing that can be said for them is that when swamped or capsized, the bark will still float, enabling the occupants to cling to the remains, at least briefly. Hanging on to a swamped sheet of bark is not an activity that merits the name seafaring, and in the shark-invested waters around the Australian coastline and in the crocodile-infested rivers of the north it is not conducive to survival. Such canoes were until recently in use here and there by Australians as these craft could be very quickly constructed. But today where the natives use canoes, those made of bark have been replaced by the dugout canoe.[2] No Australian would willingly have ventured very far from land in a bark canoe, and therefore, as we said earlier, the crossing of open stretches of ocean by the first Australians on their migration down from Asia through the Indonesian islands must have been accidental and involuntary, by being blown or carried on, whether they liked it or not. In short, they finally reached the Australian coastline as castaways drifting in from the islands to the northwest or north.[3]

When they arrived on the North Australian coast, their sea wanderings were over, for they possessed no boats which could carry them onward to the far-off Pacific Islands. These first human occupants of Australia had to make the best of the inhospitable country they found. They moved into the large, empty land mass before them and their descendants remained there without much alteration in their way of life for succeeding millennia. Those who stayed near the coast or found rivers to settle along retained the use of crude bark canoes, while those who reached the desert interior forgot about them entirely.

Such a pattern of reasoning brings us to the final question: Why were these Australians left isolated from the influence of later migrants who came by way of the same series of islands? The answer is that all later migrants—whose descendants we know today as Melanesians, Polynesians, or Micronesians—had much better canoes when they left Asia. Hence they could control where they went and had greater freedom to move on further if they did not like an area where they had landed. Evidence seems to suggest that the bulk of these later peoples, and certainly the Melanesian peoples, came from the direction of Southeast Asia around the *northern* side of New Guinea

---

[2] Lloyd Warner and others have established that the Australian tribes along the northern coasts learned about dugouts from Malay visitors in relatively recent times. (Warner 1937)

[3] See Andrew Sharp who has recently demonstrated this to be true for the Pacific generally. (Sharp 1957)

and therefore never approached the northern coasts of Australia at all, being carried on past the eastern end of New Guinea toward the Solomons and the New Hebrides. If any such later peoples did sight or land on the northern coast of Australia, they stayed only briefly, leaving no trace, probably because the region appeared uninviting. More recently, others have also found the northern coastline of Australia unattractive; these include the Japanese Navy, in World War II, which carefully by-passed it and followed the route of the Melanesians along the northern shores of New Guinea, through the Bismarcks and the Admiralties toward the Solomons and Guadalcanal. Thus the early Australians were left in isolated possession of an empty continent during the fifteen thousand or more years following their arrival.

For those who maintain that human progress is an inevitable movement, it should be noted that all the evidence indicates that during those long centuries the Australians remained at almost the same technological level as they were when they first landed.

Australian Culture When the White Men Came

The continent of Australia varies a good deal in such matters as climate, rainfall, and amount of vegetation, but in general it may be said that well over half of it is country in which keeping alive is fairly easy, even for people of such a low level of culture as that represented by the first Australians. In particular, there were no dangerous animals (except snakes), and much of the climate being like that of Southern California, the country was mostly free of tropical jungles and the diseases that are associated with them. For a primitive hunting and gathering people, the main problem of existence in Australia was lack of water, as indeed it still is today, despite modern technology. At least one-third of the continent, comprising about a million square miles, is arid desert or semidesert where rain rarely falls, and the so-called river beds are bone dry for years at a stretch.[4] Elsewhere there are well-watered areas which provide an adequate food supply for a hunting and gathering people. The Murray River Valley in the southeast and the coastal strips along the east, southeast, and north coastlines are the best watered regions, and these were the areas that supported the largest native populations when the white man arrived. But even in such favorable tracts the population was spread very thin. The best estimate of size of the native population for the whole continent before the arrival of Europeans is that within the total area of approximately three million square miles there lived slightly above a quarter of a million people, giving an average density of one person to every twelve square miles. Since over one-third of the continent is almost waterless and could support, then or now, very few humans, the density for the livable parts is more re-

---

[4] It rained in Alice Springs in Central Australia on New Year's Eve, 1929-30. According to their parents, white children six to seven years old were then seeing rain for the first time in their lives.

alistically estimated at about one person to six and a half square miles, and for the best watered sections as about three persons to every ten square miles.[5] Some detailed corroboration for this last figure is supplied by the Tiwi of Melville and Bathurst Islands who are dealt with at length in this monograph. The Tiwi are one of the few tribes occupying a well-watered and favorable environment for hunting and gathering who have been left in continuous occupation of their native habitat down to the present day. A careful and exhaustive census of them (by Hart) in 1928-29 showed that the approximately 2900 square miles comprising the two islands were occupied and used by 1062 people.

Thus between the time of their first arrival and approximately 1770 when the white men first got to know them, the original group of primitive castaways had multiplied to a population of between 250,000 and 275,000. This relatively small number (for the size of the continent) was thinly spread over most of the land, but was more numerous in the areas where the water supply was good and where the natives had available adequate sources of meat—marsupial, reptile, and bird—and fish, as well as a considerable quantity of wild plant foods.

Basically, all Australian tribes had cultures of the same general type, although local variation had developed as the original emigrants spread out into different geographical environments and their descendants lost contact with each other. The question of how many tribes there were at the beginning of white settlement is almost impossible to answer since "tribe" in Australia meant little more than a group of bands with a distinct language. There were at least five hundred distinct languages (all belonging to the same linguistic family, but most of them mutually unintelligible) which in the total population of a quarter of a million gives an average of about five hundred speakers for each distinct linguistic group. This seems a low figure for a so-called tribe and is probably brought about by the large number of very small linguistic units ("tribes") which early writers report in some areas such as coastal New South Wales and parts of Victoria. Certainly the linguistic units ("tribes") which survived down to modern times and could therefore be studied by twentieth-century anthropologists, such as the Arunta, Murngin, and Tiwi tribes, were considerably larger than five hundred people, but probably even the biggest "tribes" did not exceed two thousand in population.

Scattered in small local groups (bands) over enormous areas of country and armed only with boomerangs, crude stone-pointed spears, and spear throwers, the Australian natives were in no position to resist the white settlers. They were simply brushed aside by the early British colonists[6] who began arriving in 1788, and in the course of the next century and a half, the natives

---

[5] Radcliffe-Brown 1930.

[6] There is an interesting link between American history and the first white settlement in Australia. Prior to the Revolutionary War, Great Britain deported her worst criminals to convict settlements in the colony of Georgia. After American independence, she had to find a new dumping ground to relieve the overcrowding in the British jails and established her new convict settlement at Botany Bay near the present city of Sydney on the east coast of Australia.

disappeared entirely from much of the landscape. Since the British settled first in the well-watered fertile areas of the east and southeast, it was the tribes of these regions who disappeared earliest, so that in the present state of Victoria which once contained a comparatively dense native population, an aborigine at the present time is about as rare as a full-blood Indian in Massachusetts and for much the same reasons.

White settlement in Australia since Cook's discovery of the fertile southeast corner has tended, however, to be very localized and uneven. The lack of water in the desert and semidesert areas has continued to hamper or inhibit white occupation. Moreover, even in some places where the rainfall is relatively high, such as the northern and northwestern coastlines, isolation has continued to make these regions unattractive to any heavy white intrusion. In American terms, such lands have remained until the present day as frontier areas ("The Outback" is what the Australian city dwellers call them) and in such regions the native or aborigine ("abo" in Australian slang) can still be found, often in surprisingly large numbers and in many cases still practicing and adhering to many of the traditional customs of his ancestors. In the central desert regions the western neighbors of the Arunta continue to practice something not far removed from their aboriginal tribal life on land which the white man regards as useless for settlement purposes. Further north, in the area called Arnhem Land, on the western side of the Gulf of Carpentaria, there exists an enormous stretch of inaccessible but not at all hopeless country in which the whites have shown very little interest and in which native tribes such as the Murngin (studied by Lloyd Warner) still retain much of their traditional culture. Similarly, to the west of Arnhem Land, along the coastline and on islands lying offshore, isolation and lack of white settlement have permitted a number of tribes to continue down to the present time relatively untouched by European influences. Since the annual rainfall along the northern coast is appreciable and reliable, some of these tribes live in country that is much more favorable to hunters and gatherers than is the desert area inhabited by the Arunta and their neighbors. Among these north-coast tribes the people occupying Melville and Bathurst Islands and who call themselves Tiwi have twice been studied by modern anthropologists—by Hart in 1928-30 and by Pilling in 1953-54. The brief account which follows is presented with two main objectives in view: first, to explain how this Australian culture operated as a going concern in aboriginal times, and second, to analyze what has happened to it as it was brought into contact with the modern world.

Tiwi Marriage

Cultural Isolation

P EOPLE WHO LIVE in the congested cities and towns of the modern world have difficulty in realizing how different life can be at the hunting and gathering level of human existence. The basic fact about the life of hunters and gatherers is the thinly spread-out manner in which they live and the isolation of families and households from each other. In the case of the Tiwi, these conditions of isolation and dispersal were accentuated by their island habitat. Melville and Bathurst Islands lie off the northern coast of Australia some fifty to eighty miles from Darwin, which is the administrative capital of the empty north. They are separated from the mainland by about twenty-five miles of open sea at the narrowest part. This distance is slightly greater than the distance that separates England from France at the Straits of Dover, and just as the dim outline of coastal France can be seen from England on clear days, so the dim outline of the Australian mainland can be seen from the southern edges of the islands. However, Tiwi tradition is firm and certain that before the white man's arrival there was no contact between the islands and the mainland. To them, the dimly seen coastline of Australia was *Tibambinumi,* the home of the dead, to which all Tiwi souls went after death. It follows from this they they regarded the inhabited world as composed of their own two islands, and on those islands they lived a self-contained and exclusive existence. Occasionally outsiders appeared, either castaways from surrounding areas, including presumably the Australian mainland, and in recent centuries, fishing boats and pirates from Indonesia, loosely called "Malays" in the literature. To such visitors from outside, the Tiwi were consistently and implacably hostile. Their own traditions and what little written history there is of "Malay" penetration into the Arafura Sea both tell the same story. Outsiders who landed on the islands were massacred or vigorously resisted. Whether they were classified as *Malai-ui* ("Malays") or *Wona-rui*

(Australian aborigines from the mainland) they were not Tiwi and hence not real people, or at least not human enough to share the islands with the chosen people who owned them.

Thus, the word "Tiwi" did not mean "people" in the sense of all human beings, but rather "we, the only people," or the chosen people who live on and own the islands, as distinct from any other alleged human beings who might show up from time to time on the beaches. This exclusion of outsiders from real "us-ness" and hence from real "human-ness" was continued when the Europeans began to arrive in the early nineteenth century, and certainly as late as 1930 the Tiwi continued to call and think of themselves as Tiwi, *the* people, and to use other words for all non-Tiwi, whether they were mainland aborigines, Malay fishermen, Japanese pearl-divers, French priests, or British officials, who penetrated into their exclusive little cosmos.

Their firm tradition that the twenty-five miles of ocean were adequate to isolate them from the mainland is confirmed by certain objective distributional evidence. Several characteristic features of mainland native technology were absent on Melville and Bathurst Islands, notably the spear thrower and the curved (or return) boomerang. To anthropologists, the idea of an Australian tribe lacking spear throwers and curved boomerangs is almost a contradiction in terms, and the only feasible explanation is isolation and hence failure of these mainland traits to diffuse to the islands.[1]

That no culture stands absolutely still in its technology no matter how isolated it may be is suggested by the fact that the Tiwi, while lacking the spear thrower and curved boomerang of the mainland, elaborated their wooden spears to a complexity of design and a degree of decoration unknown on the mainland, and also developed a much greater assortment of straight throwing sticks, made of hardwood, than any mainland tribe. Moreover, their carved and elaborately painted grave posts are unique among Australian tribes, and point up both the Tiwi isolation from the mainland and the favorable food situation which permitted the leisure time necessary to manufacture the elaborate posts as well as the elaborate ceremonial spears. In the nontechnological aspects of their culture we find in many respects the same absence of mainland traits and the same elaboration of traits that were distinctively or even uniquely Tiwi. Male initiation ceremonies on the mainland focus upon circumcision or subincision or both; neither custom was practiced by the Tiwi, who instead included in their initiation ritual the forcible plucking out of the pubic hair of the novice. The degree of plural marriages achieved under their marriage rules was far greater than anything reported for the mainland; the absolute prohibition of any female, regardless of age, being without a husband was unknown elsewhere in Australia; certain features of the kinship system fail to conform to any of the mainland norms, and so on. Wherever we look in their culture we get the strong impression of an Aus-

---

[1] A toy spear thrower, played with by children, was in use, but this may be the result of post-white contact. Its native name—*pani*—seems most un-Tiwi, and a likely guess is that it was introduced by Cooper's mainlanders, being accepted as a toy for children but scorned as childish by the adult men.

tralian tribe that was able to develop within the general Australian type of culture a number of distinct features, some of them unique, while at the same time lacking entirely other features which were widespread on the mainland. Tiwi isolation from the mainland explains the differences and the lacks; their favorable environment explains why they were able to develop certain traits along their own unique lines.

The Tribe and the Bands

Because they were isolated and few outsiders came near them, they did very little as a united tribe. Everybody on the two islands was a Tiwi, and the Tiwi world stopped at the water's edge. Fuzziness on the edges of tribal territory—a chronic headache to anthropologists working with mainland tribes —did not exist, nor did the problem of marriage outside the tribe. All Tiwi, of course, spoke the same language and practiced the same customs and regarded themselves as *the* people; these were almost the only respects in which they could be said to do anything as a tribal unit. There was no tribal government, there were no tribal officials, and no occasions which required the whole tribe to assemble together as a collective entity. For daily and yearly living, the important group was the band or horde,[2] of which there were nine. The total area of the two islands is about 3000 square miles, but some of this is swampy, some of it waterless, some of it mosquito-infested mangrove jungle, and the suitability of the rest for native living varies a good deal. Hence, the actively used and lived-in areas for each band probably averaged about two hundred square miles each and, in any case, there was not a very close relationship between band size and area occupied. Details of band size at various times are given in a later chapter, but, typically, Tiwi bands probably varied in size between a hundred and three hundred people.

The band was the territorial group with which a man most closely identified himself. Though the band lived from day to day spread out over a wide area and a man might not see many of his fellow band-members for weeks at a time, the average Tiwi thought of the two or three hundred square miles of band territory as his "own country" and of his fellow members as his own people. This is why the tribal name—Tiwi—so seldom needed to be used at home on the islands. It did not identify one group as distinct from another, since all locals were Tiwi. Just as in a New York suburb one does not say that there are some Americans in the house next door, but may say that there are some Texans or some Californians or some people from Michigan next door, so a Tiwi, seeing a group of visitors arriving in his band territory, would immediately identify them as Malauila or Rangwila or by whatever band they belonged to. A father would say casually, "I have betrothed my daughter to a

---

[2] Radcliffe-Brown, the great authority on Australian tribal society, tried to introduce the word "horde" for the Australian local group, but probably because of its suggestion to the popular mind of a dense concentration of people, it has never become established and in these pages we have used the more neutral word "band."

Tiklauila" or "My wife is a Munupula woman"; a mourner would say, "He died when visiting the Munupula and therefore we will have to go to Munupi for the funeral"; an old man would reminisce about being brought up as a youth by his mother's brother, who was a Turupula, and the good times he had in Turupi; and another would recount details of big battles between the Munupula and the Malauila. All of these were band names or band territories. The nine bands thus acted, psychologically, as small tribelets or semisovereign groups, since it was with one of them that every Tiwi most closely identified in his day-to-day life on the islands. It is only when, as nowadays, he leaves the islands to go to work for the white man in Darwin that he has to think of himself as a Tiwi, since there he mingles with men of other tribes. Even then, work and residence in the white man's town does not entirely obliterate band identification. A Tiklauila in Darwin prefers to work with and to consort in the evenings with other Tiklauila, and Malauila with Malauila.[3]

Because of certain peculiar features of Tiwi domestic life, to be discussed below, it is difficult to sum up the Tiwi band in any simple formula. People, especially women, changed their band residence frequently in the course of their lives, and being born into a band did not at all require permanent residence with that band, either for males or for females. Thus the district (for example, Tiklaru or Malau) was a firm, fixed, known quantity, but the people who "owned" the district (for example, Tiklauila or Malauila) were a flexible and constantly shifting collection of individuals.

The territorial boundaries between bands were clear and well known to everybody, though they were not the sharp lines on a map such as we regard as essential for a frontier or a land boundary. All pieces of country— clumps of jungle, stretches of grassland, sections of thick woods—had names. One such piece of country, say a thickly wooded area, belonged to one band, while the more open country that began where the woods thinned out belonged to another; thus the boundary was not a sharp line but a transitional zone— perhaps of several miles—where the change from trees to open savannah became noticeable, with the band territories thus fusing into one another rather than being separated by sharp lines. The Tiwi, so to speak, thought of the landscape as a sort of spectrum where a man moved gradually out of one district into another as he passed from one type of horizon to the next. Since rivers, and even Apsley Strait, a very narrow arm of the sea separating Melville from Bathurst Island, usually have similar types of vegetation on *both* sides or banks, none of the island rivers nor Apsley Strait was a boundary or frontier between bands. The Mandiimbula, predominantly a Melville Island

---

[3] In the early 1930's the situation at the Government Hospital in Darwin offered a good illustration of this. The hospital authorities said they gave preference for house-boy jobs to "Melville Islanders because of their greater intelligence and reliability." In point of fact, some of the younger Tiklauila had established a monopoly on hospital jobs and no Tiwi other than a Tiklauila was ever hired there. The whites thought they were hiring Tiwi but the Tiklauila saw to it that they hired only Tiklauila and felt no vestige of obligation to other Tiwi to help them get these desirable jobs. The alleged greater intelligence of the islanders was undoubtedly due to the fact that the Tiklauila, having had a Catholic mission in their territory since 1911, were more used to white requirements.

tribe, owned also the country on the opposite side of Apsley Strait at the southeast corner of Bathurst, while the Malauila, the band in the northern half of Bathurst Island, conversely overlapped their ownership across the strait to take in a thin strip of coastline on the northwest corner of Melville.

These details illustrate the fact that the band was the land-owning, workaday, territorially organized group which controlled the hunting, the food supply, and the warfare. Until the white man arrived in force in the coastal waters of North Australia, the average Tiwi regarded the nine bands as the main functional units of his existence, and his loyalty to and identification with his band were given much greater opportunity for exercise than any loyalty to or identification with the whole Tiwi tribe. He did many things as a member of a band, but he did little as a member of a tribe. Only when an outsider turned up did he need to think of himself as a Tiwi, and outsiders were very rare. For the rest of the time he thought of himself as a member of his band, thought of his band as his people, and of his band territory as his country.

The Household

Since the band consisted of anything from one hundred to three hundred people, it could not live together in one place, except for very short periods of time. Hunting and gathering in almost any part of the world (except the northwest coast of America in pre-white times) require the human population to disperse itself very thinly over the countryside and live from day to day in small hunting and camping units. Such small primary groups are usually in one sense families and in another sense households, and this is the case among the Tiwi. We propose to call such units households rather than families for reasons that will soon become apparent. It is true that Tiwi "houses," especially in the long dry season (from March to October), were the flimsiest and most temporary of structures, but the group of people in question was the group who lived together day after day, hunted as a unit, pooled the results of their food getting, and ate and slept together. Functionally this group is identical with an American household, even though the "house" they used was nothing more than a few piled-up tree branches, used as shelter for a night or two and then abandoned. Like the American household also, the Tiwi household usually consisted of a man, his wife (or wives), and their children, though in many would also be included a few leftovers or extras, common to all cultures, such as bachelor uncles, visiting cousins, ancient widowers, and ambiguous "men who came to dinner" and were still there. (Tiwi households did not, however, include maiden aunts, female orphans, or ancient widows, since these could not exist in Tiwi culture.)

Thus the Tiwi household was more or less the same thing as the Tiwi family group, but Tiwi family organization had such a number of unusual twists that we find it desirable to insist upon calling such a group the household rather than the family. There was no ambiguity about its "living together" aspect; there were many ambiguities about its kinship aspects. To some of these unusual domestic usages we now turn.

Marriage by Betrothal

In many nonliterate societies, including most, if not all of the mainland Australian tribes, there is a tendency to believe that the main purpose in life for a female is to get married. The Tiwi subscribed to this idea, but firmly carried it to its logical conclusion; namely, that all females must get married, regardless of age, condition, or inclination. They (and they almost alone among human societies) took the very slight step from saying "All females *should* be married" to saying "All females *must* be married." As a result, in aboriginal times there was no concept of an unmarried female in Tiwi ideology, no word for such a condition in their language, and in fact, no female in the population without at least a nominal husband. Their own explanation of this unique situation was connected with their beliefs about conception and where babies come from. Anthropologists have long been aware that the Australian aborigines generally (and indeed some of the Melanesians, such as the famous case of the Trobriand Islands) ignored the role of the male in human conception and firmly believed that a woman becomes pregnant because a spirit has entered into her body. The Tiwi were no exception, but went a step further than the mainlanders in dealing with the dangerous situation created by the unpredictability of the spirits. Since any female was liable to be impregnated by a spirit at any time, the sensible step was to insist that every female have a husband *all the time* so that if she did become pregnant, the child would always have a father. As a result of this logical thinking, all Tiwi babies were betrothed before or as soon as they were born; females were thus the "wives" of their betrothed husbands from the moment of birth onward. For similar reasons, widows were required to remarry at the gravesides of their late husbands, and this rule applied even to ancient hags who had already buried half a dozen previous husbands in the course of a long life. It can readily be seen that these rules—prenatal betrothal of female infants and immediate remarriage of all widows—effectively eliminated all possibility of an unmarried female from Tiwi society. They also eliminated any possibility of an unmarried mother or a fatherless child. No matter where the unpredictable spirit chose to create a baby, whether it was in the body of a pretty young woman, a toothless old hag, or a little girl of six or seven, the pregnant female would have a husband, and the children when born would have a father. The Tiwi were thus probably the only society in the world with an illegitimacy rate of zero.

The practical application of these two unusual rules had certain unusual consequences. The rule of prenatal betrothal obviously gave a great deal of power to the person with the right to betroth, and in Tiwi this right belonged to the husband of the pregnant woman. We carefully say "the husband of the pregnant woman" rather than "the father of the child" because the right resided in the male head of the household at the time of the birth. Although he was ordinarily both the father of the child and the husband of its mother, there were naturally occasions when a child was born after the death of its father, in which case the right of betrothal unquestionably belonged to the mother's new husband. The clearest statement of this rule is to say that the right of betrothal of all newly born females resided in the husband of the mother at the time of the girl's birth. "He who named the child bestowed it."

In most human societies the proportion of males and females in the population is approximately equal, except in the older age-groups where women predominate owing to their tendency to live longer than men. The Tiwi conformed to this norm biologically, but their cultural insistence that all females of every age be married resulted in further unusual features of the domestic situation. No such compulsory marriage was required or expected of males. Hence, the total female population, but only part of the male population, was married. Mathematically this permitted, indeed required, a high degree of plural marriage. The men who held the right to betroth—namely, the fathers of the female babies—could, within certain limits imposed by the kinship system, bestow their about-to-be-born or newly born daughters where they wished, and they certainly did not bestow them on about-to-be-born or newly born males. On the contrary, they bestowed them, generally speaking, where some tangible return was to be anticipated. Put bluntly, in Tiwi culture daughters were an asset to their father, and he invested these assets in his own welfare. He therefore bestowed his newly born daughter on a friend or an ally, or on somebody he wanted as a friend or an ally. Such a person was apt to be a man near his own age or at least an adult man, and hence perhaps forty years or so older than the newly born baby bestowed upon him as a wife. Or, the father might bestow an infant daughter on a man—or some close relative of such a man—who had already bestowed an infant daughter upon him, thus in effect swapping infant daughters. Obviously, the fathers who did the swapping, even if they were not quite the same age themselves, were bound to be many years older than the infant wives they thus received from each other. Or, thirdly, a father looking for a suitable male upon whom to bestow his infant daughter's hand might decide to use her as old-age insurance—in which case he selected as her future husband not one of the older adult men who would be old when he himself was old, but a likely looking youngster "with promise"; that is, a youth in his late twenties or thirties who showed signs of being a good hunter and a good fighting man, and who was clearly on his way up in tribal power and influence. Such a youth, in his late twenties at the time of betrothal, would, with luck, be in his prime as "a big man" in about twenty years—a time when the father of the infant daughter would be getting old and decrepit and much in need of an influential son-in-law who was obligated to him.

There were other bases upon which infant daughters were betrothed, and indeed the father was seldom an entirely free agent, since he not only had to make his choices for his daughters within the limits imposed by the kinship system, but he was also caught in an intricate network of previous commitments, residual interests, and contingent promises made by other men who had had some prior interest in the baby or the mother of the baby. To mention only the most common limiting situation of this sort, the mother of the baby might have been given to him in the first place on the understanding that when she grew up and had a female baby it was to be bestowed on so-and-so or even returned as a *quid pro quo* to its mother's father, either as wife or as ward.

We have oversimplified the situation, but it should be clear that Tiwi fathers, in an overwhelming number of cases, bestowed their infant daughters on husbands a great deal older than those daughters. It is hard to strike an average, but the overall situation is best expressed by saying that no Tiwi father, except in the most unusual cases, ever thought of bestowing an infant daughter upon any male below the age of at least twenty-five. Taking this lowest limit for illustration, this meant that a youth of twenty-five had his first wife betrothed or promised to him at that age but had to wait another fourteen years or so before she was old enough to leave her father's household and take up residence and marriage duties with him. By this time he was about forty and she was fourteen. An age gap between husband and wife at least as great as this, but usually greater, was a necessary and constant result of the Tiwi betrothal system.

No Tiwi young man, then, could expect to obtain his first resident wife through betrothal until he was well into his thirties, at which time this first resident wife would be around fourteen, having been betrothed to him at her birth or before. But it was likely that his first wife's father, who spotted him in his twenties as a "comer," was not the only older man to want him as a son-in-law. As in our own culture, where the first million is the hardest to make, so in Tiwi the first bestowed wife was the hardest to get. If some shrewd father with a daughter to invest in a twenty-year-old decided to invest her in you, his judgment was likely to attract other fathers to make a similar investment. As a result, for *some* Tiwi men, the arrival in residence of the first wife, an event for which they had to wait until their late thirties, was quickly followed by the arrival in residence of a second, third, and fourth (at least), all of them bestowed very shortly after the bestowal of the first. Thus a successful Tiwi, having had no resident wife at all until his late thirties, would accumulate perhaps half a dozen between his late thirties and his late forties as his various betrothed wives reached the age of puberty and joined his household, and from then on he was practically certain to accumulate still more wives as later bestowals grew up and as he was able to invest the daughters borne by his first crop of young wives in transactions which brought in a later crop.

That this is not an exaggerated or overdrawn picture of the number of wives that could be accumulated in the course of a long life by a successful

Tiwi household head is shown by the genealogies of the grandfathers of the present generation. Turimpi, who was born in the 1830's and died in the early 1900's, was at his death the most powerful old man among the Tiklauila. Some of his sons are still alive, and all of them were in the prime of life around 1930.[4] A complete list of Turimpi's wives, not all of them living in his household at the same time or necessarily alive at the same time, contains more than twenty names. But Turimpi was outshone in this regard by several of his contemporaries in other bands. A prominent Turupula of the same generation had a list of twenty-five; the father of Finger of the Wilrangwila had twenty-nine; the father of Tamboo and Puti had twenty-two. As late as 1930, men with lists of ten, eleven, and twelve wives were still plentiful, and Tu'untalumi, who was aged about seventy in that year and was a man of great influence, had by then accumulated no less than twenty-one.[5]

Such numbers of wives as these per husband are very much higher than usually prevail even among the most polygymous hunting tribes. Obviously, a domestic unit with twelve or more wives in it makes for a very large household. Among the Tiwi, a household even of such men as those just named did not contain all these wives at the same time, mainly because of the very great variation in the ages of a man's wives. As far as bestowed or betrothed wives were concerned, such wives arrived at their husband's household to take up wifely duties therein when they reached the age of about fourteen. Hence the first of them to arrive (typically when their husband was nearly forty) would be women of nearly forty by the time the latest of them arrived (typically when the husband was well into his sixties). Even when the husband died, let us say at the ripe old age of seventy-five, there would probably be some of his bestowed wives still under the age of fourteen who were as yet too young to join his household. Tu'untalumi, the man of twenty-one wives, was already about seventy in 1930, yet in his list of twenty-one wives five were still ali'inga—that is, little girls not yet approaching puberty—and two were still babies at their mothers' breast. On the other hand, some of his earliest bestowed wives, who had taken up residence with him when he was in his late thirties, were already dead.

Because of this wide variation in the ages of a man's wives, it is necessary to distinguish between a "list" of a man's wives and those actually in residence in his household at any given time. The resident or active wives— one might almost say the working wives—were always fewer than the listed wives. This would necessarily be so even if marriage by betrothal were the only way by which a Tiwi man could obtain a wife. But while it was the most prestigeful form of marriage and the only respectable way in which a man could obtain a *young* wife, there were other ways of setting up a household

---

[4] See Hart 1954.

[5] Finger, Tamboo, and Puti were elders prominent in tribal affairs at the time of Hart's fieldwork. Puti was still alive in 1953-54 and well known to Pilling. Tu'untalumi, held in great affection by Hart, but anathema to the Mission Station, died in 1935.

The most important way is one which we have already mentioned—namely, widow remarriage.

Widow Remarriage

To become "a big man" a Tiwi had, among other things, to accumulate a lot of wives. This required time, in addition to everything else. A rising star who accumulated by bestowal seven or eight wives by his middle forties and then died, merely left a lot of widows to be redistributed at his graveside, and by the process of wealth attracting more wealth, or capital creating more capital, these widows were most likely to be redistributed among his rivals and competitors of his own age group or among men even older than he. Hence, the largest number of wives ultimately accrued to the successful man who lived longest, since he was likely to gather up at least a few of the widows of each of his contemporaries or seniors as they predeceased him.

There was thus a close correlation between increasing age and the number of wives a man had, and the largest households belonged to a few surviving old men in each band. The two conditions, therefore, which were necessary to accumulate a large household were (1) to attract prospective fathers-in-law to invest their infant daughters in you while you were a young man, and then (2) to live long enough to reap the dividends. The longer you lived, the more dividends would accrue to you from one source or another, provided you started off right by attracting betrothals in your twenties and thirties.

But what about the unimpressive young men, the "noncomers," who somehow failed as young men to attract any prospective fathers-in-law to invest an infant daughter in them? As we have seen, even the most highly regarded and well-connected Tiwi young man had to wait until his late thirties or longer before his first bestowed wife was old enough to join him in domestic bliss, but at least while waiting he knew the time was coming. The overlooked or unbetrothed young man had no such prospects. Since the only source of supply of new females was through the birth of female infants whose hands only their fathers could bestow, it would appear as if a young Tiwi male overlooked or ignored by all fathers of bestowable female daughters had no alternative except permanent bachelorhood. Doubtless Tiwi fathers, as a class, would have regarded this as an ideal situation and would have said that permanent bachelorhood was a proper fate for such friendless and hence useless young men, but no social system of such rigidity has ever been discovered by anthropologists. Tiwi fathers were able rigidly to control the marriages of their infant daughters, but they were not able to control with the same rigidity the remarriages of their own widows, and it was widow remarriage that supplied the loophole in the system, or the cultural alternative that took care of young men.

A Tiwi husband was unavoidably and necessarily always much older than a bestowed wife. Therefore he usually died much earlier than she. A girl of fourteen who entered into residence with her first husband when he was fifty was likely to be left a widow by him within the next fifteen years, and even if she remarried a man of the same age as her first husband, she could easily be widowed for the second time while still herself a comparatively young woman. There were several different patterns, most of them intermingled in the same household, for a female matrimonial career, but the situation may be illustrated by the concrete case of one of Turimpi's widows, an ancient crone (in 1930) named Bongdadu. Born about 1865, she was betrothed at birth to a powerful old man named Walitaumi who was at least the same age as her father, if not older. Not unnaturally, he died while she was still a child and well before she was old enough to join his household. Her betrothal was then reassigned, so to speak, to Walitaumi's half-brother, Turimpi, then in his early forties. About seven years later, she joined Turimpi's household as a blushing bride of fourteen, her husband then being close to fifty. In the next twenty years she became Turimpi's most prolific wife and bore numerous children, three of whom, Antonio, Mariano, and Louis, all born between 1883 and 1900, were men of importance in Tiwi politics in 1930, and one of whom, Louis, is still alive today.[6] Around 1900, when Bongdadu was still only about thirty-five, she passed to M., a middle-aged Tiklauila, and was his wife until his death around 1925. By this date, Bongdadu was over sixty and had borne ten children, four of whom died young. Not unnaturally, she was beginning to approach the hag or crone stage of Tiwi womanhood. Nonetheless, she had to remarry, but by now all of the people who might have claimed any rights of bestowal in her were long since dead, her eldest sons were adult men of some importance and able to protect their mother's interests, and clearly she was unlikely to produce any more children.[7] Her chief value was as a food producer and housekeeper and female politician, roles for which she had been well trained in her long years as wife of Turimpi and M.

Old women in Bongdadu's position had to remarry, but they were in a good position to exercise some choice of their own as to whom they remarried, especially if they had strong influential sons to support them in their wishes. There was a frequent pattern in such cases for the widow, aided and abetted (or perhaps even forced) by her sons, to arrange a marriage of convenience with some obscure nonentity much younger than herself and usually a friend or contemporary of her sons. In 1925, then, Bongdadu, widowed three times already, married as her fourth husband one Dominico, a man of no importance whatever, as was shown by the fact that at this time he was nearly forty and had not been able to attract even one bestowed wife. He had, however, already married one widow, so that his marriage to Bongdadu gave

---

[6] Tiwi personal names are polysyllabic and hard for the reader to remember; hence, wherever possible, we have used "whiteman names" for individuals. The frequency of Spanish names among these "whiteman names," such as Mariano or Dominico, derives from the fact that the original buildings for the Mission Station were built by a number of Filipino workmen whom the priests brought with them.

[7] The Tiwi saw no inconsistency between believing in spirit impregnation and believing at the same time that an old woman was unlikely to bear children. It was to them a matter of probabilities, and of course with them as with us, occasionally an elderly lady did—disconcertingly—have a baby, proving the logic of their position.

him a second wife, also, of course, a widow. This marriage is of further interest when we discover that Antonio, Mariano, and Louis, the main sons of Bongdadu by a previous marriage, had some influence in arranging this marriage of their mother to a contemporary and satellite of theirs, and that a year or two before, Antonio had married the ancient mother of Dominico when *she* became a widow. In other words, Antonio and Dominico had married each other's mothers; Antonio while waiting for his oldest bestowed wife to grow up, Dominico with no bestowed wife in sight. The approximate ages of the parties at the time of these marriages were:

Antonio	37	Dominico's mother	55
Dominico	38	Bongdadu (Antonio's mother)	60+

Earlier, we mentioned the practice of fathers swapping their daughters within the infant bestowal system; here we find sons swapping their mothers within the widow remarriage system.

This is a relatively simple example of the complexity of Tiwi domestic arrangements, and we hesitate to complicate matters further. But clearly the last remarriage of Bongdadu (to Dominico) and the remarriage around the same time of Dominico's mother to one of Bongdadu's sons, a friend of Dominico, raise some important issues of social structure, particularly the question of whether widow remarriages of this type are to be regarded as a subspecies of bestowal marriages, with the sons having a right of bestowal over their mothers parallel or similar to the right of bestowal possessed by fathers over their infant daughters. Space does not permit any adequate discussion of this fascinating theoretical issue, but we can point out two factors which strongly deter us from regarding Tiwi widow remarriage as a special case of bestowal marriage. One is the self-evident and empirically observed fact that Tiwi widows, who remarried as Bongdadu and Dominico's mother remarried in the quoted case, were usually highly vocal and pretty tough old ladies who were not easily pushed around by anybody, even by their adult and ambitious sons. Whom they remarried in their old age was a matter upon which they had themselves a good deal to say. Secondly, to any anthropologist familiar with the kinship structures of Southeast Asia and the Pacific countries, there is a great deal of difference, in a society with matrilineal clans such as the Tiwi had, between a father making marriage decisions for his daughters, who do not belong to his clan, and sons making marriage decisions for their widowed mothers, who do belong to the same clan as their sons. We prefer, therefore, to view the overall Tiwi marriage situation and the interrelationship of their two forms of marriage as essentially a system wherein the matrilineal clan had lost its right to make marriage decisions for its female children, that right having been taken over (usurped) by the fathers of those children. The daughters of the clan were disposed of, not where fellow clansmen decided, but where an outsider (the father) decided—thus, bestowal or betrothal marriage. But when the female no longer had a father—that is, when she was old and could only be remarried through widow remarriage—then the right of her clansmen and more specifically her sons (in consultation with her own wishes) to arrange her remarriage became restored as a sort of residual or reanimated right. Moreover, as we shall see, it was in line with their own political interests for the sons to insist on exercising such a right.

Naming Rules

Such a way of integrating the two forms of marriage is supported by the Tiwi rules for naming children, which are very relevant to the issue. We mentioned earlier that the right to bestow a daughter was vested, strictly speaking, not in the actual father, but in the man who named her. Personal names were important in the Tiwi value system[8] and were given to every child a few weeks after its birth by its father or the man currently married to its mother. But whenever a husband died and the widows remarried, all the personal names given to their children by the dead man became strictly taboo, and the new husbands of the widows had the duty (or right) of providing all the children with new names. Since most women were widowed several times in their lives, most children were thus renamed several times in *their* lives, and the names given them by the earlier husbands of their mother dropped completely out of use.[9] Logically under this system nobody would get a permanent name until his or her mother was dead, since as long as she were alive she would remarry and her new husband would rename all her children, no matter how aged they might be. The Tiwi insisted that logically this was how the naming system was supposed to work, and, in fact, the personal names of even prominent senior men did become taboo whenever their mothers' current husbands died. But convenience proved stronger than logic and the personal names of most men and women became well established in their early adulthood as people became used to them. While such names did become taboo when the man who had given them died, the taboo in such cases was temporary rather than permanent, and after a decent interval the name would creep back into use replacing some new and unfamiliar one which might be bestowed by the widow's new husband. In general, the name which thus became permanently or irrevocably attached to a person was the name which a person held when he or she first emerged into tribal prominence or first began to get talked about. For a male, this was most usually the name he was bearing in his late twenties and early thirties; for a female, the name she was known by in her early adolescence when she first left her father's household to take up residence with her earliest husband.

That convenience thus overbore logic in the Tiwi naming system by

[8] See Hart 1931.

[9] It can easily be seen what headaches this naming system created for an anthropologist trying to collect genealogies. Individuals would occur in one genealogy under one name and in another under another name, making the task of cross-indexing and cross-checking enormously difficult.

attaching some one semipermanent name to a person despite the rules of name taboo should not cause us to overlook the importance of these rules. In theory, at least, every new husband renamed all his wives' children by all their previous marriages—thus, at least symbolically, canceling out the signs of title of all the previous "fatherhoods" in those children and asserting his own fatherhood right as a new and exclusive one. A widow's new husband was the new household head for all her children, and he took over this position by renaming them all, thus becoming their legal father. If we can stop thinking of "father" as a biological or kin relationship, and think of the word as meaning only "head of the household," the Tiwi concept will become understandable. We will also realize that there is no contradiction or illogic involved in the Tiwi beliefs that male parents were not necessary for conception, but that every child born must be born to a woman with a husband. All they meant was that every child must be born into a household with a male at its head who belonged to a different clan from its mother—in other words, a "father," in Tiwi context.

The renaming of the children by the new household head was not, of course, sufficient to wipe out the commitments made by previous titleholders. Although the new father could and did change his step-daughters' names, he could not change their bestowals. The men upon whom the daughters had been bestowed by the previous father made sure of this. The new father was compelled to carry out the marriage arrangements for the daughters made by his predecessors in the fatherhood role, and there was sure to be a terrific row if he tried to alter them. Nevertheless, he acquired some power over the future of the daughters. The man to whom one of them had been promised by the previous father might die, thus making redisposal of the girl possible for him, or some new deal might be arrangeable in which he could use his new assets— for these new step-daughters were assets, regardless of the fact that their immediate matrimonial future was already settled. The new father could delay his decision as to whether they were yet old enough to join their betrothed husband or even drop a few hints that he did not think the betrothed husband's right to them was quite as certain as was generally believed. Such actions, of course, were liable to lead to violent reprisals by the betrothed husband, but there was always a chance that he would be open to a deal; for example, by giving an option on one of the women in whom he had an interest, he would seek to hasten the appearance of the girl in his own household or seek to clear whatever shadow upon his title to her the step-father sought to cast. Even the last husband of an elderly widow who had already passed through the hands of six or eight husbands and all of whose daughters were grown up and married two or three times already, gained some shadowy rights in the future remarriages of those daughters by marrying their ancient mother. And the validation of these shadowy rights was the fact that as their mother's new husband he had renamed the daughters and he who named them could bestow them. The only catch was, that while he could wipe out all the names bestowed by his predecessors, he could not equally readily wipe out their commitments. All he could do was maneuver within the network created by their commitments so as to try and advantage himself as much as possible by a skillful use of whatever shadowy right in the daughters he had obtained by becoming their current "father."

It is within such a context that the apparent swapping of mothers by Dominico and Antonio must be viewed. By marrying Bongdadu in her dotage, Dominico had acquired some rights in the future remarriages of her daughters, the sisters of Antonio, but since his marriage to her had been, partly at least, arranged by Antonio and her other sons, he would have to share with them his disposal rights to their sisters. Similarly, the marriage of Dominico's ancient mother to Antonio (part, so to speak, of the same "package deal") meant that Antonio as current father had some say in the future disposal of Dominico's sisters when they became widowed, since he had the power of renaming them.

What in effect occurred in this, as in many other cases, was that men of different clans and of about the same age formed a partnership or close alliance wherein "sons" and "husbands" cooperated in arranging the remarriages of their "mothers" and "sisters" by acting as quasi-fathers and treating their mothers and sisters as "quasi-daughters." The partnership or "firm" of Dominico (of the Crane clan) and Antonio, Mariano, and their brothers (of the Red Paint clan) had already arranged the remarriages of Bongdadu (Red Paint clan) and of Dominico's mother (Crane clan), and stood ready to take care of all future remarriages of any of Bongdadu's daughters (Red Paint) or Dominico's sisters (Crane) whenever any of these women became widowed. Each member of the firm was trying to maximize his own self-interest in this and all the other alliances he had a share in, but operations had to be carried out in this partnership form because the marriage of any woman had to be arranged by her "father," and the father, in the Tiwi rules, had to be a non-clansman of the woman whose marriage he arranged. Hence the Red Paint men needed Dominico, a Crane, as a front man to arrange the remarriages of their sisters, and he in turn used Antonio, a Red Paint man, to arrange the remarriages of his sisters. When clansmen made decisions about the remarriages of their sisters, they could only do it by using agreeable nonclansmen as nominal "fathers" and cooperating with them—and the agreeable nonclansmen would of course only come in on the deal if there was something in it for them, as there was for the obscure and unimportant Dominico in the present case. In return for acting as a front for the Red Paint brothers, he got himself a second wife, an excellent food provider though no longer beautiful; he became the ally, even if junior, of some men with assured futures; and he acquired some shadowy residual rights in the future remarriages of several potential widows. Dominico did himself a lot of good by marrying Bongdadu; if he hadn't married her, he would never have attracted much tribal notice and hence would not have warranted mention in these pages.

We find that the whole complex situation makes most theoretical sense if we see it as essentially an institutional struggle between clan rights and the father's rights in women. Tiwi fathers, as suggested above, had taken away from the clan the right to make marriage decisions for newly born female members of the clan. As mechanisms validating this success of father's rights against clan rights there existed two rules: he who bestowed the name had the right to dispose in marriage; and all names given by a woman's previous husband were cancelled by his death and a new set of names given to all her children by her new husband. Strictly and universally enforced, such rules would put *all* control over the marriages of *all* women, of every age, in the hands of their mother's husbands—that is, men from outside the clan of the women being disposed of, in other words, fathers in the Tiwi sense. But the Tiwi system failed to achieve such a result though their rules are pointed toward it. They achieved something close to it as far as infant or even young girls were concerned, since the fellow clansmen of such girls were either (as brothers) too young and unimportant to have any power to resist this alien control over their sisters' hands, or (as mothers' brothers and hence older men) too involved and absorbed in their own activities *as fathers* to take any position asserting clan rights as against fathers' rights. To be successful in tribal life, an ambitious young Tiwi male was best advised to forget his mother and his sisters' daughters (all members of his clan) and concentrate on getting wives for himself. Only by getting wives could he have daughters, and only by having daughters could he build alliances and obtain influence, power, and more wives. To get wives for himself, he could not use his mother or his sisters or his sisters' daughters, since their disposal was in the hands of the men who had named them—that is, their fathers. But there came a time in the life of an older man when his mother was old, and *her* mother was dead, and therefore the rights of the last man to name his mother had lapsed. And a similar situation would arise in the case of his sisters when their mother's last husband died. By this age, a man so situated was likely to be powerful enough and skilled enough in the rules of the game to exert some control over the late remarriages of his elderly sisters and even of his mother, were she still alive. Whenever this occurred, although the resulting situation might have the superficial appearance of clan solidarity—with sons, mothers, brothers, and sisters all acting and planning together as a partnership—such a surface appearance was illusory. The motivations involved in it were scarcely altruistic desires on the part of the brothers to look after their mothers and elderly sisters, but rather efforts by the brothers to use to advantage, in their intricate political schemes, some women of their own clan (their mothers and elderly sisters). Earlier in life these men had been prevented from such manipulation by the control over those women exercised by nonclansmen (their husbands or fathers) through the naming rules. Put another way, we might say that Tiwi men as a group had acquiesced to the system wherein "the father" had control over all marriages of his "daughters," because every Tiwi man hoped to be a "father" himself; but having acquiesced, every Tiwi male tried to beat the system, especially as he became older and more influential, by intriguing in the remarriages of his mother and elderly sisters—matters in which, according to the strict letter of the law, he had no right to interfere, since bestowal rights resided with the "father" or "fathers" of these women. One factor which greatly contributed to the setting aside of the rights involved in the naming system was the fact that since, on the whole, old men married young women and young men married old women, in many cases the nominal "father" of an elderly woman was very much younger and less influential than were her brothers, or her sons by an earlier husband. The brothers and/or sons, there-fore, were able to override the wishes of their sisters' nominal father since the seniority system was on their side in such contests, even though the renaming rules were not.

Although it was very rare indeed for any Tiwi male to have a resident young wife until he was nearly forty, long before that age he was likely to acquire an ancient widow or two. In at least ninety out of every hundred cases a man's first resident wife was a widow very much older than himself. Accord-ing to a complete genealogical census carried out in 1928-29, nearly every man in the tribe in the age group from thirty-two to thirty-seven was married to an elderly widow. Many of them had two elderly widows and a few had three. But very few of them, and certainly not more than one out of five of them, had a resident *young* wife. About half of them had bestowed wives, but these were mostly toddling infants who would not come into residence with them for another ten years or more. Even for the most promising and rapidly rising young man, the first young bestowed wife was not likely to arrive until several years after his marriage to a widow.

To get a start in life as a household head and thus to get his foot on the first rung of the prestige ladder, a Tiwi man in his thirties had first of all to get himself married to an elderly widow, preferably one with married daughters. This was the beginning of his career as a responsible adult. The widow did several things for him. She became his food provider and house-keeper. She served as a link to ally him with her sons. As her husband, he acquired some rights in the future remarriages of her daughters when they became widowed. And she, as the first resident wife in his household, stood ready to be the teacher, trainer, and guardian of his young bestowed wives when they began to join him after they reached puberty.

Levirate, Sororate, and Cross-Cousin Marriage

We have emphasized infant bestowal and widow remarriage because it was the elaborate development of these two matrimonial mechanisms that brought about the unusual, perhaps unique, character of the Tiwi household. Other matrimonial mechanisms, more usual in preliterate societies, were also used by the Tiwi but always in combination with or as minor adjuncts to the two basic mechanisms. Thus, a man often remarried his dead brother's wives, or at least some of them, within the institution of widow remarriage. Such a practice is known to anthropologists as the levirate, and tribes are said "to have" the levirate or "not to have" it. The Tiwi, with their pluralistic approach to the whole area of marriage relationships, can hardly be said to fall into either category. To them, every widow had to remarry and among the many possible candidates for her, the brothers of the dead husband were recognized as having a reasonable, but far from automatic, claim. Whether the brothers

jointly, or any one of them singly, were able to translate that claim into marriage depended on the other claims. Brotherhood in itself gave no exclusive
right to widows, but of course a brother, being necessarily of the same clan
and frequently of the same band as the deceased husband, was well in line
to assert a claim to the widow if he could make the claim good. Cursory inspec-
tion of the genealogies reveals, however, a surprisingly small number of cases
of men taking over the widows of their deceased brothers. At best it was a
very minor factor in Tiwi marriage customs.

The parallel custom of the sororate—that is, of sisters being married
to the same husband—was more common. It occurred both in connection with
infant bestowal, by a father promising *all* his daughters by a particular wife
to the same husband, or in connection with widow remarriage, whereby two or
more full sisters, previously married to the same husband, passed together
on his death to the same new husband. The sororate occurred more frequently
in the first form than in the second, largely because, as already mentioned,
widows had more say in their own marriages than baby girls had, but there
was nothing obligatory nor required about it, as is shown by the frequent
cases in which a father bestowed all his daughters by one wife on the same
man but on the early death of that man rebestowed them *seriatim* on several
different husbands. One got the impression, though no Tiwi ever made the
point explicit, that within the Tiwi bestowal system the prevailing high rate
of infantile and child mortality was an important factor in sustaining the sororate principle to the extent that it did exist. A father who bestowed upon a
man the first daughter borne by a certain wife was almost obliged to bestow
upon the same man the second daughter of the same wife if the first one died
in infancy. Moreover, since most fathers bestowed their daughters with an eye
to their own advantage, it was clearly desirable if he wanted to cement the
goodwill of a prospective son-in-law, to promise him *all* the daughters produced by a certain wife, so that even though most of them died in infancy, at
least one or two would be delivered in good condition at the age of puberty.
The aim of bestowal was to win friends and influence people, and a bestowal
of a child who died before she reached the son-in-law did a father little good.
A shrewd father could avoid this risk by following the sororate principle;
a stupid or feckless father who scattered his daughters widely could well end
up with as many disappointed sons-in-law as friendly ones, as the infantile
and child mortality took its heavy toll of his young daughters. In the genealogies, sororate marriages in some form occur much more frequently than
levirate marriages, but nonetheless their incidence is such as to indicate that
they were a relatively minor feature in Tiwi marriages and that their occur-
rence was most frequently due to careful fathers trying to insure sons-in-law
against disappointment, and themselves against charges of nondelivery.

No account of marriage in any Australian tribe can go very far without
raising the difficult matter of the kinship system, since all the accounts we have
of mainland Australian tribes tell us that all marriages there took place within
a rigid kinship framework which required everybody to marry somebody who
was automatically his or her cross-cousin (for example, a man and a daughter

of his mother's brother).[10] Enough has been said already to indicate that in Tiwi marriage nothing was automatic. Females were given in marriage by their fathers, or (to a lesser extent) by their brothers, or (to a still lesser extent) by their sons. But fathers died and were succeeded by the men their widows remarried, and these men renamed all the widow's children, and by renaming them established some rights to make marriage decisions for the females. Therefore, cross-cousin marriage in Tiwi was merely part of the total system of marriage and had to adjust itself to the rest of the system. In theory, fathers could only bestow their infant daughters on men who stood to them in the relation of sisters' sons. Conversely, every man who received a bestowed wife received her from a man who was technically his mother's brother and of course the girl's father. To this extent the Tiwi were a tribe who practiced cross-cousin marriage and their kinship system belonged to one of the commonest Australian types, that which Radcliffe-Brown called Type I, having investigated it among the mainland tribe called the Kariera.[11] But a kinship system of the Kariera type could not accommodate all the complexities that had been introduced into Tiwi life by the emphasis on infant bestowal and widow remarriage. In particular, the generations kept getting badly mixed up, as for instance in the very common case of old men bestowing their infant daughters on other old men of their own age group, and in return receiving as infant wives (or wards) daughters of those old men. With this happening constantly, it was difficult to maintain the kinship principle that recipients of wives were always sons of the donor's sister and donors were always brothers of the recipient's mother. Which was mother's brother and which was sister's son in the case of two old men busily swapping daughters was a problem that put a severe strain on a Kariera-type kinship system. And widow remarriage introduced further complexities. We have already mentioned the case of two young men, Antonio and Dominico, who through a judicious use of widow-remarriage had ended up married to each other's elderly mothers. This was no isolated case; many pairs of men of like age were married to each other's mothers. Who called whom "father" and who called whom "son" became an insoluble riddle in such cases.

To avoid further involvement in the labyrinthine complexities of Australian kinship organization, all that we need say here is that the Tiwi had unscrambled the potential confusion introduced into their kinship categories by inventing a few new terms which, superimposed upon their Kariera-type system, kept everything straight. In Kariera, and generally among all the mainland tribes, no kinship distinction was made between potential wife and actual wife or between potential "in-laws" and actual "in-laws." A Kariera male called all the girls who were eligible for marriage to him by the same term (*Nuba*, usually translated mother's brother's daughter); all the fathers of such girls

---

[10] The definitive work on Australian kinship systems is Radcliffe-Brown 1930-31, and there is a large technical literature on the subject. See also Elkin 1951; Berndt 1955 and 1957; Murdock 1949.

[11] See Radcliffe-Brown 1913.

by the same term (*Kaga,* usually translated as mother's brother); and all the mothers of such girls by the same term (*Toa,* usually translated father's sister or mother's brother's wife). When he married one of these girls he still called her *Nuba,* he still called his wife's father *Kaga,* and still called his wife's mother *Toa.* But not in Tiwi. For them, all potential wives were, in theory, mothers' brothers' daughters and all potential wives' fathers were mothers' brothers. But when a man married any such girl, he immediately called her by a new and different kinship term which can only be translated as "wife," and corresponding new and separate terms were used for the actual wife's father, actual wife's mother, and even for the actual wife's father's sister. Thus marriage introduced for a Tiwi a new set of relatives with new kinship terms different from those he used toward his general run of cross-cousins, mother's brothers, father's sisters, and so on, and these "relatives by actual marriage" terms, being based on actual marriages rather than kinship categories, were capable of handling in a fairly orderly manner all the complexities introduced into Tiwi domestic life by such customs as old men exchanging infant daughters or young men marrying each other's mothers. We may sum it up briefly by saying that Tiwi marriages operated within a general framework of cross-cousin marriage kinship categories identical with the categories of the Kariera, but that females had become such important assets in power and prestige relationships among the senior men—marriage had become, so to speak, such a political affair—that a new set of kinship terms based on actual marriages had to be superimposed on the terms geared to cross-cousin marriage; in cases of conflict or anomaly or confusion in the cross-cousin terms, the terms based on actual marriages were controlling or took precedence. Which is only another way of saying that in theory all Tiwi marriages were rather idealistically approximated to marriages between cross-cousins, but in practice they departed quite far from such an ideal; so far, in fact, that extra kinship terms had been introduced to take care of the relationships created by such departures.

"Disputed" Wives

There is still one more category of wives to be mentioned, a category for which the Tiwi had no name in their own language but which in pidgin English they referred to as "stolen" wives. A few women so labeled were likely to turn up in the "list" of the wives of most big men, but analysis of the circumstances in each case makes it clear that "stolen" was an unsuitable label and that wives so designated were most often in a status that should be called either "disputed" or "shared." In legal terms they were wives in which there was or had been a divided interest. To explain fully the nature of these cases would carry us over into both the Tiwi legal and sexual systems, and here we are trying to confine our analysis to those aspects of marriage that have consequences for household organization. Since these disputed or shared wives had to at least reside in some household and had at least a nominal current husband at any given moment of time, all we need to note about them at this point is that in any listing of a man's wives we have to include "disputed" wives in addition to all the other categories of wives mentioned previously.

The Household: An Overview

In the discussion so far we have selected only those aspects of the Tiwi family complex that had close bearing on the nature of the household. These aspects can be briefly summarized as follows:

1. the high number of wives per husband that a successful man was likely to acquire if he lived long enough.

2. the two distinct mechanisms by which wives were acquired—infant bestowal and widow remarriage.

3. the operation of the bestowal system in such a way as to prevent even the most promising young man from achieving coresidence with a bestowed wife until he was at least nearly forty years old.

4. the tendency for success to lead to more success, whereby *some* astute men received into their households a number of young wives in rapid succession after the age of forty.

5. the tendency of younger men and of nonbetrothed younger men in particular to marry elderly widows while waiting for betrothed wives to grow up or, in the case of those with no bestowals in sight, to enable them to start a household of their own.

6. as a result of the integrated operation of all these customs, the strong tendency in Tiwi households for husbands to be very much older than their wives (as a result of infant bestowal) or very much younger than their wives (as a result of widow remarriage) or—what was commonest of all in the bigger households—some combination of both. Hence many a Tiwi husband had some wives much older than himself, including some already dead (but still counted), and some very much younger than himself, including some who were still babies in their mothers' wombs (with their sex still undetermined). All these dead wives, current wives, nominal wives, "disputed" wives, not-yet-joined-the-household wives, and not-yet-born wives were still counted in a husband's list, and the length of his list was a measure of his influence, power, and importance as a household head.

It is now perhaps clear why we chose to begin our account of Tiwi culture with some discussion of Tiwi marriage. Compulsory marriage for all females, carried out through the twin mechanisms of infant bestowal and widow remarriage, resulted in a very unusual type of household, in which old successful men had twenty wives each, while men under thirty had no wives at all and men under forty were married mostly to elderly crones. This unusual household structure was the focal point of Tiwi culture. It linked together in an explicable unity the kinship system, the food-gathering system, the political and prestige system, the totemic system, the seniority system, the sexual system, and the legal-moral-religious system of the tribe. Or perhaps all these should be labeled as subsystems under the household structure, the master system which unified them. We turn therefore to consider the Tiwi household as it affected the food-gathering and leisure-time activities of the people.

2

Life in the Bush

Organization: Band and Household

THE PRECEDING CHAPTER should convey something of what a Tiwi band really was. The casual way in which people left one band and joined another shows that the band was in no sense a tight political or legal group. Old men preferred, on the whole, to bestow their daughters on men in other bands, but far from this indicating any tendency towards patrilocality, there was at the same time a strong tendency on the part of such selected sons-in-law, especially if they were young and mobile, to move into the band of the father-in-law, partly, at least, to ensure that the donor did not change his mind. Even the faint prospect of a wife was sufficient to cause young men to change bands, and change of band residence by senior men was not at all rare.

The emphasis on widow remarriage was another factor that influenced band residence and made the whole matter of band affiliation extremely fluid and arbitrary. For widow remarriage not only caused elderly women to move perhaps several times in their lifetimes, but also caused their younger sons to move with them. Such unmarried sons preferred home cooking and followed their elderly mothers outside the band if remarriage required the widows to move. Almost invariably the question "Why is So and So (a youth of 15-25) living in Turupi if he is really a Malauila?" evoked the response (obvious to a Tiwi) "Because his mother is there." Conversely, mothers often followed their sons, especially when the son began to acquire young wives who needed senior female supervision. Such mothers divided their time between the household of the son (or even several sons) and the household of the nominal husband, and if such part-time residence in two (or more) households involved part-time residence in two (or more) bands, the arrangement did not provoke any comment, nor was it thought to be in any way odd.

The fluidity of band affiliation was so constant a feature of Tiwi life that almost the only firm generalization that can be made about it is that when "a big man" with a large household had lived most of his adult life in the territory of a band, and had been up to the time of his death one of the dominating elders of that band, his children, both male and female, would be regarded as "really" members of that band during *their* lifetimes, regardless of where marriage took the girls, or where their own life careers or the remarriages of their mothers took the boys. Thus in 1928 the three oldest men of Malau—Ki-in-kumi, Enquirio, and Merapanui—were regarded as core members of the Malauila band. Reference to their family trees reveals that the latter two had been born in Malau to a big man of that band in the previous generation and had resided in Malau all their lives. Ki-in-kumi, however, always thought of as equally a Malauila, in fact had been born in Rangu to a Rangwila father and had moved to Malau as a youth when his marriage prospects had seemed to him best in that district. This move had happened so long ago that only old people remembered it, and as a result all three old men were generally regarded as "real" Malauila and the children of all three would so be regarded all their lives. Such identification would hardly carry over for more than one, or at best, two generations. In explaining the matter, we have had to use the English word "really" in quotation marks because the Tiwi themselves had no corresponding concept. If one asked "Why is he a Malauila when he never seems to live there?" the answer would be "Because his father was, and he grew up there." It was only in pidgin English that one could talk of a "real Malauila" or a "real Rangwila." In Tiwi language and thought, Malau or Rangu was a firm, fixed, unchanging piece of country; the Malauila or Rangwila were the households, of constantly changing personnel, who hunted there, and a man had to belong to one of those households practically all his life and have his father before him also a permanent resident of the same district before his identification with that district was sufficiently close to approximate the degree of identification that is implied in the European concept of a "real" Malauila or "really" a Rangwila.

The crux, then, of Tiwi territorial organization was not the band but the household.[1] A band was merely the temporary concentration in one district of semiautonomous households which were the food-collecting, living-together, and sleeping-together units of Tiwi life. People were not members

---

[1] There has been a prolonged argument in the anthropological journals about the Australian territorial unit, especially as to whether it was patrilineal or matrilineal. For the Tiwi, such a problem could not arise. A father bestowed his daughters where he wished and at puberty they joined their husbands. Where his sons found wives was no concern of the father, and hence where they established their households was of no interest to him either. The father would wish, however, that they would establish their households as far away from his as possible since then he would not have to worry about them interfering with his young wives. On the other hand, it was thought to be "unfatherly" actually to throw sons out. See G. P. Murdock and A. R. Radcliffe-Brown and A. P. Elkin in *American Anthropologist* (*passim*) for the main contributions to the mainland argument, which we think becomes pointless when dominance of the household ties over band ties existed, as it did among the Tiwi.

of bands as part of any political or legal system; they were members of households as part of a domestic system. What held the unit together was the central position and dominance of the father or husband, and hence the life of a household was only as long as his lifetime. When he died, the household broke up and the surviving members joined other households, perhaps in the same district, perhaps in some other band territory. Such change of household was carried out by the individuals concerned, not quite at will, but certainly not with sufficient uniformity for any political or legal label to be put upon it.

Uniformity was derived from the fact that every Tiwi had to live in a household. The universal prohibition on unmarried females was obviously one expression of that requirement. For men, the requirement was less firm, and if a young man wanted to live entirely alone he was free to try—although there is no record of any man having tried it for more than a few weeks at a time. Even if his mother were dead and his father or step-father did not welcome him, he attached himself to some household since, apart from any question of loneliness, this was the only way by which he could eat regularly. For Tiwi households were primarily autonomous food-producing and food-consumption units. A household made its own decisions, camped where it saw fit to camp, moved on when the food quest made it advantageous or necessary to move on. A large household, such as that of Ki-in-kumi or any other big man, was a complete community in itself, with the old man as executive director. He laid down the daily, weekly, and monthly work and travel schedules for the women, the young men, and the children. Most of the time the work went automatically because all the adults and the older children knew their jobs.

Daily Activities

By shortly after dawn each day, the household was up, and after a light breakfast, usually of leftovers from the previous night, everybody left camp to go to work. The women and children (except perhaps the five- to ten-year-old boys, who were rather useless at that age) scattered in every direction from the camp with baskets and/or babies on their backs, to spend the day gathering food, chiefly vegetable foods, grubs, worms, and anything else edible. Since they had spent their lives doing it, the old women knew all about gathering and preparing vegetable foods, and they supervised the younger women. This was one important reason for men marrying widows, and even a man with many young wives was quite likely to remarry an elderly widow or two nonetheless. A husband with only young wives might have a satisfactory sex life, but he still needed a household manager if he wished to eat well. The supervision of the female members of the household was left to the old women and, provided the returns were good, the husband did not attempt to interfere nor to give orders concerning the details of women's work.

After the women had scattered out in a wide circuit from the camp, the husband might hunt, but only if he were not too old. In hunting kangaroos,[2] wildfowl, and other game, keen eyesight is essential, hence Tiwi men did very little hunting once they were past about forty-five, though they hated to admit their hunting days were over. The meat, fish, and game provided for the large household of an old man was obtained by the young men, and this was about the only thing an old man thought his sons or his step-sons were good for. Typically the young man, when he returned at nightfall with a kangaroo which he had spent most of the day tracking down and spearing, would ignore the old man and dump the carcass at the feet of his mother as if to say, "I brought this back for you, not for that old So and So."

As the women straggled back to camp toward sundown with the results of their day's gathering and the young hunters brought in their bags, cooking began and the main meal of the day (usually the only hot meal) was eaten. The Tiwi themselves had no doubt about the close relationship between plural marriage and good eating. "If I had only one or two wives I would starve," the head of a large household once told the missionary who was preaching against plural marriage, "but with my present ten or twelve wives I can send them out in all directions in the morning and at least two or three of them are likely to bring something back with them at the end of the day, and then we can all eat." This was a realistic appraisal of the economic situation and it is to be noted that he put the emphasis on the food obtained by the women gatherers rather than that supplied by the male hunters. Based on the observations of 1928-29, it would appear that the Tiwi ate pretty well, especially in the larger households. Kangaroo and other marsupials, and some of the larger lizards (for example, the goanna) were very plentiful in the bush, as were fish and turtles and dugong on the coasts and wild geese in many districts. But all these were extras or dividends; the staple everyday foods were the vegetable foods gathered day after day in apparently unending quantities by the women. For most months of the year there was always plenty of *kwoka*, a porridgelike dish prepared by soaking and mashing the small nuts of a native palm. These nuts grew in such quantity that in every large camp baskets or dishes of *kwoka*, at various stages of preparation, were always available, even for midnight snacks if anybody woke up hungry. *Kwoka* was about as dull and tasteless as Scotch porridge, but equally filling, and naked small boys full of *kwoka* had stomachs distended like balloons. In the wet season the place of *kwoka* was taken by *kolema*, a yam whose ripening and growing season was much shorter than that of the nuts from which *kwoka* was made. It was on the abundance of the *kolema* yams during January and February that the Tiwi supported the more elaborate of their collective ceremonials.

The abundance of these and other vegetable foods, plus the ample supply of game and fish in many places, meant that under aboriginal conditions the Tiwi lived at a food-consumption level much further above the near-

---

[2] Actually there are no kangaroos on Melville and Bathurst Islands; the chief meat animal is a slightly smaller species of marsupial technically called the wallaby. As the distinction is important only to zoologists, and as many of the so-called kangaroos in American zoos are in fact wallabies, we prefer to use the more familiar word.

starvation level than was the case with many of the mainland tribes.[3] Even to talk about the Tiwi in near-starvation terms seems quite incongruous, for there was an abundance of native food available the whole year around and their only problem was to collect or catch it. We regard the development of their large multiple-wife household as essentially their own evolutionary solution to the problem of finding the most efficient unit of food production. Abundant food was there in the bush in its raw state; the most efficient way to extract it was by a work unit represented by such households as those of Ki-in-kumi, or Tu'untalumi, with the old remarried widows directing the young women and the hunting and fish spearing being done by the younger males.

Even the smallest households nearly always contained at least one old female veteran of the food quest who knew the bush like the palm of her hand and could wrestle some food out of the most inhospitable district. The only households that ever went hungry—and they only overnight or at worst for twenty-four hours or so—were the small households of only one or two wives, especially if both wives were young and inexperienced or young and flighty or both. Such households were uneconomic and were rare. On the other hand, the apparently absurd households such as those in which two young men shared their respective elderly mothers as wives, made good economic sense. Any attempt by two such young men to substitute two young wives or even four young wives for the two old ladies would have drastically reduced the standard of living of the household. When young wives arrived in Tiwi households they were not regarded as replacements for the old crones but joined as reinforcements and apprentices to the skilled workers—the veterans. The sexual aspects of marriage were necessarily subordinated to the housekeeping or food-production aspects, which is why in the previous section we spoke of every young man laying the foundation of his household by marrying an elderly widow usually long before there was any young wife in sight.

Since the bigger the household the more food it produced for its own consumption, there was a tendency for the smaller and therefore hungrier households to hang around the fringes of the bigger ones. Though every household was autonomous and could camp and collect food anywhere in the band territory in which it roamed, it was rare to find all the households in a band distributed evenly over the available territory. In Malau, Enquirio's household and that of Merapanui were usually to be found camped together, since the two men were full brothers and not in competition with each other. Also camped with or near them on any given occasion would be a few other small households. Such a combined group as this would, all told, amount to between forty and fifty people camping at the same spot and remaining together for weeks at a time. Under mainland conditions in most areas, a gathering of forty people for ten days at a time in the same locality was unheard of, except on

---

[3] As was pointed out earlier, the best-watered and most fertile areas of the mainland were the areas attractive to white settlement, and the tribes who inhabited such areas (for example, Victoria or coastal Queensland) were wiped out quickly. Most of the mainland tribes who survived long enough to be studied by modern anthropologists were tribes whose habitats were unfavorable both for native and for white occupation.

special rare ceremonial occasions, because of the poverty of the food supply. The prevalence of such large camps among the Tiwi supports our general thesis that their native food supply was, for Australia, unusually plentiful, and that, in this sense, the Tiwi were a "rich" Australian tribe.

When camped together thus, the various households kept their distance, with the main fires and shelters of each separated by some twenty or thirty yards from the others, and during the day when everybody (except the old men) was out food collecting, the camps were almost deserted. When the food gatherers returned in twos and threes in the late afternoon, each household would cook and eat at its own fires as a unit, but if they wished, members of the smaller households, in which food returns for the day were probably smaller per capita than those of the bigger households, would "drop in during supper" upon the latter and supplement their own slender meal. Such hospitality was always extended on an individual basis; some member of the bigger household, usually a senior wife, would offer to one of the visitors a piece of meat or a dish of *kwoka* and if rebuked by her husband she would justify her act by mentioning her own kin relationship to the visitor, as if to stress that the kindness was her own individual gesture and did not commit the whole household to friendliness. Heads of large households were, however, generally very permissive if such handouts were made by senior females of their household to women or children of other households; it was handouts to adult male outsiders, especially young male outsiders, that were likely to provoke snarls or reprimands from the old man. This was in line with the general hostility of all old men to all young unmarried men that ran through all aspects of Tiwi culture.

After darkness fell, such a camp, with three or four households all resting within easy hearing distance of each other, became highly animated with men visiting from fire to fire as the women, who were not encouraged to walk about after dark, gossiped around their own fires. Little productive work could be done after dark, though a few cooking chores and food-preparation activities were performed, and most people went to sleep early unless the shouted conversations from fire to fire earlier in the evening had started an argument. If an argument did arise, the participants might go on abusing each other at long range for hours, with many of the listeners becoming involved and the rest remaining awake to enjoy the row.

Such rows were almost invariably outgrowths of the constant suspicion with which older men regarded younger men. This suspicion was in turn part of the price the Tiwi had to pay for the efficient type of food-production unit that they had evolved. This production unit, to reach maximum economic efficiency, required the vast majority of all females to be concentrated in the households of a very small number of husbands; namely, the very oldest men. As a necessary correlate, men under twenty-eight had no wives at all and very few men under forty had any wife except elderly and physically very unattractive widows. The efficient economic organization thus obviously created a moral and social problem—the problem of how to keep the unmarried young men away from the young women. The old head of the household had a double role:

he was at the same time the executive director of a work unit which he expected to work for him, and the husband of many of its members whom he expected to be faithful to him. The young wives were willing, under supervision, to meet his first expectation, but found it difficult, even under the strictest supervision, to meet the second. Successful supervision of the morals of young wives was easy to achieve at night because each camp was then gathered together and it was relatively easy for the husband and his senior wives to guard the young wives closely. But during the daytime matters were different. Then the young women of the household were widely scattered through the fairly dense bush and it was impossible for the old wives to watch them every minute of the day. And the young men of other households, or even of their own household, were hunting game in the same neighborhood. Encounters, whether by chance or by previous arrangement, were likely to occur and probably occurred with a high degree of frequency. We say "probably" because no anthropologist working with a tribe which has neither courts nor written records can ever know how often casual extramarital offenses take place. (There is even some difficulty in obtaining reliable statistics on such matters in our own society, as the attacks on the late Dr. Kinsey's statistics indicate.) We therefore make no statement about how common the act of adultery was in Tiwi culture, but we can say that, judging by the public accusations of adultery, its practice must have been widespread indeed. In any Tiwi camp comprising more than two households, few weeks went by without an outraged and angry old husband shouting accusations at one of the younger men sitting by another camp fire a few yards away. The young man accused would (usually) deny it; the old women of both households would enter the argument, the young man's mother protesting his innocence, the old man's elderly wives (who had of course been the informers) giving details of time and place and circumstance; the young man would produce, or try to produce, an alibi and appeal to a friend to bear him out; the old man would call the friend a liar and the youth's mother an old witch; the youth's mother would retaliate by shouting things she knew (but had never before revealed) about the private lives of everybody in the old man's household, including the old man himself when he was a young bachelor. A good time would be had by all, including the listening anthropologist, but nobody would get much sleep. Such nocturnal uproars, always starting with accusations hurled by an older husband against a younger man and always involving incidents that had allegedly occurred while the young wife was somehow left unchaperoned for a short period during her daytime wandering in search of food, were a commonplace of nightlife among the Tiwi; but no case was ever reported, observed, or hinted at in which even the most adventurous and enterprising bachelor had succeeded in seducing, or had even attempted to seduce, a young wife when she was back in camp after nightfall. The deeds were always done in the secrecy of the bush during the daytime; it was the recriminations and accusations that occurred in the public glare of the campfires at nighttime.

Sometimes these disputes or accusations went no further than the nocturnal shouting of charges. Often the young man accused the previous night quietly slipped away to some other camp and was not seen the following morning. The matter might then die, depending largely on whether the old husband wanted to carry it further or was content to drop it. If the young man was still in camp the following day, the old man might insist on a duel then and there, but it would take place only if the camp were large, since Tiwi duels were essentially legal actions and as such needed a sizable audience for their correct staging. Disputes between men, of which old men accusing young men of seduction were by far the most common type, usually remained at the verbal level until a large body of spectators was available. Since such large concentrations of many households were necessary for the performance of the main collective ceremonials, it was at the time of these ceremonials that most verbal arguments were pushed by the aggrieved party to the action level.

During the dry season (April to November) when travel was easy, the only collective ceremonials sufficiently important to draw together a large number of households were those held for the funerals of big men. In the wet season (November to March) when the grass and bush were high and travel was difficult, the main collective phases of the male initiation ceremonies were held (see Chapter 4), and these brought together for a few weeks at a time large numbers of households. The funeral ceremonies for adults were always held some considerable time after the death and burial of the deceased. How long a period elapsed between the death and the funeral ceremonies depended on the expected size of the gathering, and this figure correlated, at least roughly, with the importance of the deceased. Here again the overriding consideration was food supply, since the chief mourners (that is, the deceased's closer relatives) had to feed everybody who came to the funeral while the ceremonies lasted, which might be almost a week. The more important the dead person the bigger the crowd at his funeral, and hence the greater the amount of time needed by the mourners to arrange the catering. As much as a year might elapse between the death and the time when the mourners felt that the funeral arrangements—especially the food supply, but also the ceremonial preparation—were sufficiently well in hand to permit them to set a date and send out invitations for the funeral ceremonies. Funerals, therefore, were not held at regular times but were individually scheduled at times fixed by the chief mourners. They were always held in the dry season, however (except those of young children, to which nobody came in any case), and therefore an old man who had a dispute to settle or a case to try publicly could always depend on a few big funerals being held in the not very distant future which would provide the large audience necessary to make the settlement of the dispute legal. During the wet season the kolema phases of the initiation ceremonial always drew a large attendance; the annual time of these was pretty definitely fixed by the ripening of the kolema yams.

Hence the verbal wrangles in the small scattered encampments at night, about seduction during the day, could have any one of three outcomes, depending largely upon the determination of the old man-accuser and the demeanor of the young man-accused. If by the following morning the young man had disappeared and showed no further interest in the old man's menage, the matter might end there. Or the old man might let matters rest until the time of the next big gathering of people at a funeral or at the *kolema* rituals, and then revive the issue under such public circumstances that the accused young man could not slip away unpunished. If he followed this second course, the old man went to the gathering covered from head to foot in white paint, the Tiwi uniform for anybody who came in anger and intended to pick a fight with somebody. The decision between these two lines of action lay, of course, with the old man, and while that decision was to some extent determined by how vindictive and revengeful he felt, nonetheless it was also influenced by how this dispute was related to all the other feuds, disputes, deals, marriage exchanges, and so forth, in which both parties were already involved. Like a good lawyer in our own culture, the old man had to consider, before he took the matter to court, who the young man was and who his friends and relatives were, and had to ask himself whether in seeking vengeance for the blow to his pride he might not be doing himself more political harm than the injury was worth.

In arriving at his decision, the old man was influenced to some extent also by another variable, the attitude of the young man. If the alleged offense occurred only once and the young man denied it and thereafter kept his distance, the accuser would probably let the matter drop. Offenders were very rarely caught *in flagrante,* and the evidence of seduction was almost always circumstantial or hearsay. In every case there was some element of doubt as to whether the right young male was being accused or whether the whole story had not been invented by some of the old wives out of sheer spite toward a young wife. The old man had to take such factors into consideration, not out of any abstract sense of justice, but because, naturally, he didn't like to be made a fool of, either by young men or his own spiteful old wives. But he was most suspicious and unbelieving of his own flighty young wives, and sometimes the accused young man was defiant and persistent in his attentions to the same young wife, or wives. In effect, such a young man was daring the old husband to do his worst. Such continued defiance of the seniority system could not be permitted; it became a case not of simple seduction but of subversive activity, since it was a threat to the whole social structure of the tribe, centered as that was around the marriage of old men to young women. When confronted by such action, a Tiwi elder said (as people of other cultures might), "What would happen if everybody did that? We'd have complete anarchy and free love." Hence an old husband, so defied, was almost duty bound not just to seek satisfaction for the private injury done to himself, but to defend the public weal by hauling the offender before the bar of public opinion and denouncing him before as large a crowd as possible, as a public enemy. If the situation became so flagrant that he could not wait until the next big funeral or the next *kolema* gathering, he began calling in surrounding camps or going himself, dressed in white paint, to summon them to assist him in meting out public justice to the violator of the system. When a sufficient number of upholders of the right (that is, senior heads of households) had been collected together, the usual one-sided duel (see below, Chapter 4) was staged and this was usually sufficient to incapacitate the offender and make him decide to move—at least for a while—into some other district. The group thus hastily convened to mete out public justice seldom numbered more than sixty or seventy people (seven or eight households) and having been convened *ad hoc* would remain camped together only for the forty-eight hours or less needed to deal with the emergency.

Joint Activities

This discussion of the alternative lines of action open to an outraged household head enables us to specify the relatively rare occasions during the year when the dull, quiet, day-by-day, food-gathering routines of the dispersed household camps were interrupted by events that required many households to gather together in one place and indulge in joint action. Foremost among these occasions were big funerals and the *kolema* ceremonial, both of which were mentioned above. These were the main religious events of the year, full of dancing, singing, wailing, and excitement. The excitement was the psychological result of so many people being together at the same time, a rare experience in the life of any Tiwi. Since the *kolema* ceremonial was an annual event and even the most enthusiastic funeral goer did not attend more than three or four really big funerals in the course of a year, we may reckon that even an old and important man, much concerned with ritual observances, would probably find himself a participant in such crowd activities on not more than some six occasions per year. For less important men and for women and children the number of such occasions was less than six. The *kolema* ceremonial lasted two weeks or more, big funerals, even when they became the occasion for carrying on other public business, did not last more than four or five days each. Hence we may reckon an average of about a week each for the half-dozen times a really big man spent in the company of a sizable crowd of fellow tribesmen, giving a total annual average of about six or seven weeks at most out of every fifty-two—or a little less than 10 percent of the year spent by an old important man in large ceremonial activities or what Durkheim calls the collective life of the tribe.

In addition there were the smaller gatherings, such as the funerals of younger men and most women, and the calling together of a number of households to settle a dispute in the manner we have described above. These were collective occasions also but they brought together a considerably smaller crowd. A really big man's funeral was likely to draw over three hundred people or even as much as one-third of the whole tribe.[4] Not only did many

---

[4] Tamboo's funeral in May 1929 (he died in the previous August) drew practically the full band membership (men, women, and children) of the four Bathurst Island bands; almost all the Munupula; many Mandiimbula; and large delegations from the remaining three bands. With such a crowd, an actual head count was difficult, especially of the children, but there must have been over four hundred people present. Needless to say, excitement was intense; more fights occurred, more insults were exchanged, more ancient feuds revived and new ones started, and more food consumed than at any funeral in living memory. At least that was the opinion of Tamboo's chief mourners, but since it was they who threw the party and had to pay for it, they may have been biased.

people come to such a funeral to express their kinship with, and pay their respects to, the deceased, but as mentioned above, many men with disputes to settle or fights to pick let such matters ride until the next big funeral was called and then took advantage of the large crowd to provide the necessary witnesses for the transaction of the outstanding legal business. Gatherings of many households for purely legal affairs, without funerals or *kolema* ceremonial as the main *raison d'etre* for the gathering, were comparatively rare and when they did occur they were usually called by one man, to settle one case only, and hence did not promote the attendance of very many households. Similarly, the funerals of most women and of younger and therefore less important men drew together at most ten or twelve households and a few other individuals, so that the crowd was usually not above one hundred people at the most. A single *ad hoc* legal duel, even when an episode in a long-drawn out and notorious dispute, seldom drew more than this number. Duels always attracted some spectators who came for the excitement, even though not personally involved, provided of course they were camped somewhere in the vicinity.

This second type of collective gathering, of which the smaller funerals and the single duels were the main occasions, might then require the attendance of a household head, accompanied by some or all of his household members, perhaps five or six times a year. These gatherings would each last less than forty-eight hours, and since the people the household head met at them would mostly be people of his own band or of closely adjoining bands, the excitement of seeing unfamiliar faces—people not seen for over a year perhaps—would be absent. We may reckon that attendance at these smaller, more localized gatherings, and the participation in group activity which they entailed, took up two more weeks, all told, out of the yearly round. When these two weeks are added to the six or seven already estimated for the time spent by a busy public man at the large gatherings, we find that even the busiest and most gregarious senior elders spent less than ten weeks out of the fifty-two in collective activity outside their immediate households.

To complete the list of occasions which called for joint activity by the members of several households, we must include the joint kangaroo hunt. This activity was very localized and very spasmodic, occurring only when and where conditions were right and somebody felt sufficiently energetic to organize it. Much of the Tiwi country is a mixture of dense scrub and relatively open savannah; kangaroo are relatively easy to hunt in the latter but very hard to get near in the denser types of vegetation. The native method of hunting was based on getting as close as possible to the animal before it saw or heard the hunter. If it detected the hunter, it fled, and no Tiwi in his senses ever threw a spear or a throwing stick at a moving kangaroo.[5] Only when the animal was standing still and the hunter was close enough to aim carefully at a vital part was the spear thrown. At certain seasons of the year, particularly after the end of the wet and early in the dry season, many sections of good kangaroo country gave very poor hunting returns because the grass had become

---

[5] The up-and-down movement of a hopping kangaroo in flight makes it an extraordinarily difficult target even for skilled white hunters armed with shotguns or rifles.

so high and rank that the hunters were unable to get near the kangaroo. In this event, a senior man of the district might decide to convene a grass-burning posse. To it he invited more or less whom he pleased, so long as he included other household heads of the same band and other senior men from outside it whose ancestry gave them some claim to be invited. At the appointed time the hunters assembled, perhaps ten or fifteen adult men, with younger ones doing the actual hunting and the older ones supervising. The women and children acted as beaters; the grass was set on fire over a big area, and the kangaroos rounded up and killed while dazed by the smoke and the noise. The bag of animals killed in such a concerted hunt sometimes ran higher than one kangaroo per participant, so that every man, woman, and child present was able to gorge himself on kangaroo meat for a day or two. This sudden glut of meat was not, however, the main object of the burning, but a dividend. Even though few kangaroos were caught in the smoke and confusion, the burned-over area would provide good visibility for kangaroo hunting during the rest of the dry season, since the new tender shoots that sprang from the burned-over grass were a favorite food of the kangaroo and served to lure them out of the denser scrub areas and the mangrove swamps where hunting them was always difficult.

These occasional joint hunts, like the occasional small fights and the funerals of unimportant people, usually brought together only the members of households who lived relatively close to one another, so that while they are included in the list of events which interrupted household isolation, they did not, as a rule, involve any interaction between members of any wider group than the neighboring households. Perhaps the whole matter of activity beyond the household and the band can be illustrated best by an actual case. We have already mentioned the venerable Tu'untalumi, an old man resident among the Tiklauila, who as late as 1929, and despite the fact that by then the Tiklauila were the band most subject to mission influence, nonetheless had a list of twenty-one wives. In other ways besides his record of polygamy, Tu'untalumi was a pillar of the old culture. Though past seventy and much too old to hunt, he was a most enthusiastic and indefatigable song and dance composer, and in his zest for ceremonial he made a point of attending every big festival and as many smaller ones as he could get to. The whole tribe respected Tu'untalumi as a big man, liked him as a person, admired him for his steadfast support of Tiwi traditions, and most of all accepted him as a sort of leading authority on ritual matters. When dubious or disputed points of ceremonial were submitted to him, his decision, given clearly and firmly and with much citation of precedent and the distant past, was accepted without demur. His presence at a gathering located outside his own district was always a source of gratification to the household which had convened the gathering. The fact that Tu'untalumi had seen fit to attend not only made that household feel important but also provided its members with a technical guide and arbiter for unofficial help in running the rituals. The old man loved going to parties— and he was always a welcome guest—and years of such activity had given him such a sturdy, wiry constitution that despite his near-seventy-five years he could outdance and out-sing and out-party most of the men fifty years younger than himself.[6]

Since Tu'untalumi was a senior Tiwi household head who spent more of his time attending festivals, funerals, fights, and other collective occasions than did most of his contemporaries, it is instructive to examine his movements over a full year. If he had kept an engagement book during 1928-29, it would have looked something like this:

Early April (end of wet season): Leaves his home base in Tangio where he has spent most of the wet season and visits the Mission station to attend a few small funerals (children who have died at the Mission in the preceding months). During these funerals a series of fights and duels also takes place. Total people present: perhaps fifty or sixty. Time thus spent in helping to wind up public business: five days. Returns home to Tangio and remains there for rest of April.

End of April: Goes to Rangu with a big party of other Tiklauila for a funeral (junior elder). Fairly big funeral, lots of people, lots of disputes. Time away, including leisurely journey to and from Rangu, about two weeks. Gets back home about middle of May.

Middle of May—end of June: Lives quietly at home with his household in Tangio.

About July 1st: Goes to Mission for a few days, "visits" with whoever is there. Tries out a new composition of his own (song and dance) on group camped at Mission. Returns home for rest of July.

Last week of July: Taking his younger wives and their children with two senior wives in charge of them, sets out for Malau for a big funeral with lots of people and fights. There he performs his new dance; is much consulted on ceremonial matters by the Malauila; gets into a few fights himself but handles them with dignity and honor; remains in Malau two weeks; stops off to visit and attend a small funeral with the Munupula on his way back; has a fight with a Munupula while there; returns to the Mission; stays there a day or two dispensing all the news from Malau and Munupi to those camped there; issues invitations for a grass burning in some sections of Tangio which were not burned in April or May. Goes on home to Tangio where some of his older wives have remained during his absence. Total time away: about three weeks.

End of August: Is joined in Tangio by several other Tiklauila and Rangwila households whom he has invited. Grass burning and joint kangaroo hunting goes on for four or five days. Dancing and partying at night. After five days most of visiting group leave and he and his household remain alone in Tangio until well into October.

---

[6] There is no suggestion that Tu'untalumi was in any way an official ritual leader. All old men, by virtue of their years, were to some extent ritual leaders; he had merely worked harder and longer at it than most of them. His tirelessly joyful personality had a good deal to do with his success in the self-established role. In a culture that might be thought likely to make all its men gloomy, anxiety-ridden introverts, he was a warm, happy, dignified old extrovert and he was widely admired.

Middle of October: Rains about to commence. Last chance for travel before the wet season. Goes to another district for the naming ceremony of a new baby (he is its mother's father, having bestowed the mother on the man now naming the child). Goes on from there to the Mission. Finds a large party there about to visit the Mandiimbula on Melville Island, ostensibly for a funeral but really for a big argument since Tiklauila-Mandiimbula relations were badly strained at this time.[7] Joins this party. They go in force to the Mandiimbula country. Big fight. He is not much involved in the fighting, concentrates on the dancing.

End of October: Returns to Mission. War party disbands. He returns home to Tangio and remains there until the initiation ceremonies begin in late January. During this period (November-January) makes occasional very short visits to neighboring households and is occasionally visited by neighbors who drop in on him from no great distance away.

End of January: *Kolema* phase of initiation begins. As guardian of ritual, he is in much demand by the various groups with boys of suitable age. All the Tiklauila and Rangwila households gather together (about 300 people) for nearly four weeks to conduct these ceremonies. Much feasting, much dancing, he in the center of everything. Very few fights or disputes, which is the way he likes it.

End of February: Finish of *kolema* season. Finish of ceremonies. Households disperse. He and his household return to Tangio and remain there for the balance of the wet season, which usually ends toward the end of March.

During the year for which we have listed the details, Tu'untalumi attended three big funerals, one big *kolema* ritual, and several small funerals, and made a few other miscellaneous visits to other districts. In addition, he was the host at a joint kangaroo hunt in his own district and attended the naming ceremony of one of his daughters' children. He also was a member of one war party. Although this hectic social whirl totals up to about thirteen weeks spent away from home or with a large party of guests in the home, even the busy and popular Tu'untalumi spent about thirty-nine weeks out of the year living alone with his household and seeing nobody except members of that household. Since there were few other Tiwi as gregarious as he, we may take this figure as an outside limit and conclude that the great majority of "big men" spent at least four-fifths of their time in the isolated environment of the single household, engaged largely in the daily routine of getting a living and supervising their wives and children in their unending food quest.

---

[7] We have tried to keep out of the text those factors in the 1928-30 situation which were clearly due to post-white influences, and this friction was of that order. Briefly, Mandiimbula fathers with daughters bestowed on Tiklauila husbands were failing to deliver the girls at puberty to those husbands, hoping instead to hire them out as prostitutes to the Japanese pearling boats which periodically visited the Mandiimbula and Yeimpi beaches in search of women. See Chapter 6 for a full discussion of this outside influence as well as that of the Mission, which (for different reasons and motives) was also in the girl-buying business at this time.

The mobility of people other than household heads was much less. Women and children could move only with the permission, and usually in the company, of their lord and master. Occasionally old and trusted wives might be sent, unsupervised, on a journey by their husbands or their brothers, usually to carry messages and bring back gossip, but young wives were never trusted to be out of sight either of the husband or of elderly female supervisors. Young men were less subject to their fathers' orders and hence were fairly free to come and go as they pleased, but the universal suspicion which all husbands bore toward wandering young men put severe restrictions on their mobility and prevented them attaching themselves to any household or camp in which they did not have some close relative.

The fact, then, that a man like Tu'untalumi was (in Tiwi terms) very mobile did not necessarily mean that members of his household shared his degree of mobility. When he took most of his large household with him on his journeys away from home, as he often did, it was always because he was going a considerable distance and was traveling slowly, living off the country as he went. In such cases he liked to have a large retinue to feed him on the way and also to permit him to entertain in fitting style when he arrived. For while it was true that at a funeral or at an initiation the relatives of the deceased or of the novices were supposed to take care of the feeding of all the visitors, nonetheless, wealthy and generous men like Tu'untalumi believed in taking along with them a bevy of young wives, with a couple of efficient elderly widow-wives in charge of them, to contribute to the food-getting and food-preparing activities. Of course the supervision of the young wives' morals in the strange environment was often difficult, especially in the hectic atmosphere of a big ceremonial, but this worry was compensated for by the fact that the visitor who came so attended was contributing a number of extra food providers to the labor force of the harassed hosts and thus making a generous gesture, and also by the fact that such a visitor was not dependent upon the hospitality provided by the hosts. Having his own food-producing unit with him, he could live better and stay longer than if he had come alone or only as one of a party of men. In this respect, as in so many others, a Tiwi household head's decision had to be reached by balancing against one another the two competing motives of, on the one hand, the desire to eat well and, on the other, the desire to keep his young wives safe from prowling bachelors. Ki-in-kumi, the wealthiest man of the Malaüila band, usually decided not only to leave his wives at home but also not even to go himself. But Ki-in-kumi was a gloomy, pessimistic old man. Tu'untalumi usually decided to do the thing in style, travel with a large retinue, have all the comforts of home while in strange districts, and take his chances on the strange bachelors. He clearly believed that a good booming ceremony with lots to eat and himself in the center directing the dancing was well worth the risk of a few of his young wives being seduced off-stage. Men like Ki-in-kumi thought Tu'untalumi an old fool for not leaving his young wives at home, and Tu'untalumi probably thought that old Ki-in-kumi might as well be dead, especially since his death would be the occasion for a really magnificent funeral.

The matter of men traveling to distant camps for ceremonials illuminates again, and from a new angle, the great value of elderly widows in the household. Tu'untalumi, during his visit to Malau in August, was able to split his household efficiently by taking a couple of old wives with him to supervise his young wives on the journey and leaving other old wives at home in Tangio to begin storing up food for the grass-burning project which he intended to stage on his return. It will be noticed in the account of his movements that he began issuing invitations to the grass burning on his way home from Malau, showing his confidence that the elderly wives he had left at home would have the preparations well in hand during his absence. A big man with a big household really needed three or four elderly widows because these enabled him to split his work force in various ways as his various political and social obligations required and to be sure of trustworthy supervision of each of the segments. A man without widows in his household, or with only one, could not do this; in fact, it was hard for a man without widows to attend ceremonials at all, or even to receive a large party of visitors to his household. And, as we have already pointed out, since such a man would probably go hungry very often because he would not dare to send his unsupervised young wives into the bush to gather food, there were practically no such men nor such households. Widows were indispensable to a senior Tiwi, both in his public and in his private life.

Making Things

Throughout this chapter we have been stressing the contrast between the dull routine of life in an isolated Tiwi household during the greater part of the year and the sort of life typical on those relatively rare occasions when something special—a festival, a funeral, a fight, a grass burning, a naming ceremony, some collective phase of men's initiation—required the assembling together of several households for joint activity. Before leaving the daily life of the isolated camp, we should mention one other area of activity—namely, the manufacturing activities of the tribe. The Tiwi did not manufacture much, but spears, throwing sticks, canoes, digging sticks, baskets, bodily ornaments, graveposts, and all the miscellaneous paraphernalia used in ceremonials had to be made in whatever leisure time people could find during the long weeks and months when each of the households lived more or less in isolation from the others. Crude and simple as these artifacts were, their construction required time, and only the older men had the time and the skill based on experience to make the more important of them.

Largely because of their failing eyesight, the older men hunted very little and hence tended to remain in camp all day while the young men were hunting and the women were gathering. There were, of course, some old men who took advantage of this time to do little except doze in the shade, but most of the household heads spent a fairly active day in camp engaged in making things. Here we find another aspect of Tiwi culture that results from the relatively favorable food supply. Some of the Tiwi artifacts, particularly the highly decorative graveposts and ceremonial spears, are unique among Australian tribes, and the carving and painting of these graveposts and spears were skills possessed only by the senior men. They were provided with the leisure time necessary to develop and use these skills by the efficiency in food production of the large household which all old men were expected to accumulate with age, and which many old men did succeed in accumulating. We said earlier that the bigger the household, the better its members ate. We now add the further correlation that the bigger the household, the more leisure time was provided for its head to engage in manufacturing and artistic production. Tu'untalumi has been cited as an example of a large household head (twelve resident wives and thirteen children at home in 1928-29) who loved ceremonial affairs. It would be wrong to infer from this that Tu'untalumi only loved going to parties. He also loved preparing for them, and this preparation (for him as for all other senior men) included the manufacture of ceremonial spears, the preparation of graveposts, and the composition of songs and dances. In the long dull periods between trips outside his home district, he spent most of the days and many of the nights in the creation of these ceremonial necessities. He was not a full-time specialist in the sense that he made spears or posts to exchange with other men who had neither the time nor the skill—the rules of kinship required that every senior man make his own ceremonial spears and contract for his own posts. Tu'untalumi manufactured his graveposts to meet his own ritual obligations, but he took a more magnanimous view of those obligations than did most men. Put in our terms, we might say that he was wealthy enough (in the size of his household) to be generous with his own productions. One example of this attitude was his attendance at funerals that other men of equal kinship to the deceased did not find it necessary to attend; his frequent contribution of an extra gravepost to those provided by the chief mourners of the deceased was a similar gesture. "Tu'untalumi not only came to our mother's funeral, he also made a gravepost for it" was a very gratifying reflection for an obscure group of mourners to cherish among their memories, and of course it was acts of this sort that made the old man so well liked and admired. The economic point of the matter, however, is that only a man with as large a household as his could afford the gesture of giving away, in a situation where kinship obligations did not demand it, a gravepost that required about a week's full-time work.

It was, however, sad to observe that as an artistic producer Tu'untalumi, like many intellectuals in other cultures, tended to operate in too many media. His work as a composer of songs and dances was universally admired, but his graveposts, while appreciated, were not regarded as being as outstanding, technically speaking, as those of another old man, his crony Timalarua. In personality, Timalarua, a successful household head (eleven living wives, ten children at home), was quiet spoken, placid, and only mildly gregarious, and he is mainly of interest because in his leisure-time activity he paid but routine attention to song and dance compositions and concentrated rather single mindedly on making canoes, ceremonial spears, and graveposts. Frequently, on the banks of some creek or river in Tiklauila territory, a party wanting to cross would scout around and find a canoe hidden in the weeds. Everybody would use it to cross, and the question "Whose canoe is it?" would elicit the reply, "Oh, it's always there and everybody uses it who wishes to cross." But if the question were "Who made it in the first place and put it there?" the answer would be, "Probably Timalarua. He likes making canoes; he makes them all the time." He also liked making spears and posts, though he was not as generous with them as Tu'untalumi. When one of his posts appeared at a funeral, people would point it out admiringly saying, "Timalarua made that one" and the speaker would trace the lines and designs on it with his finger, using much the same gestures as an art critic in a modern gallery. When a post by Tu'untalumi was identified and admired, however, the admiration was for Tu'untalumi the generous person rather than Tu'untalumi the artist. One was a wonderful craftsman, the other was a wonderful man. But acclaim given to the song and dance performances of the two men was just the reverse: the dances of Timalarua were adequate but not outstanding, those of Tu'untalumi were in a class by themselves.

Comparison of the activities of these two old men illustrates the impossibility of drawing any line, in the simpler cultures at least, between artistic production and technological production. The canoes and the posts manufactured by Timalarua and the posts manufactured and the new dances created by Tu'untalumi were all, so to speak, in the same category, as far as the Tiwi were concerned. The distinction we might make between the canoes as "useful" products and the posts and dances as ceremonial or artistic products never occurred to them. All were objects or products which only successful old men had the required skill and leisure to make. The fact that one old man liked to make canoes and leave them around for other people to use, and another old man liked to compose dances and perform his compositions widely for other people to enjoy, to them merely indicated individual taste and choice; it did not make the first a craftsman and the second an artist. This point has been overlooked in most of the theorizing about primitive art; perhaps a necessary first step in the development of primitive artists is for a society to be able to provide a few men with enough leisure time to be able to cultivate what might perhaps best be called hobbies, since a hobby can equally well be something "useful" to society, like canoe making, or something personally satisfying, like dancing or decorating graveposts.

The huge, heavy, painted spears made by these old Tiwi men were mainly used only for display, and even the oldest men were positive that this had always been the tradition. In fact, they seemed a little shocked at the implication that such beautiful and valuable objects could ever have been used for such mundane purposes as hunting or warfare. The cutting and painting of such spears took time and skill—more time than a gravepost—and no important man went to the smallest gathering without bearing on his shoulder at least half a dozen of these symbols of his importance. If on his way through the bush he sighted a kangaroo, he dropped his painted spears and stalked the animal with an ordinary spear, or more probably left it to the young men in the party who carried only ordinary ones. The painted spears were symbols of wealth and status and roughly corresponded to white tie and tails in our culture. No important man could afford not to have them, even though for most of the year they were unused. Before leaving home on a journey, it was often necessary for a man to renew the paint on his spears, for it rubbed off easily. Since paint was an aspect of ritual, its use, even the renewal of old paint, was senior men's prerogative; women were not supposed to touch it.[8] The analogy with formal dress even extended to the borrowing of ceremonial spears. An important man, caught short of them, might borrow some from a contemporary who had plenty, and though everybody would know that his spears were borrowed, he at least was properly dressed for the occasion, though stark naked otherwise.

Baskets made of bark with gummed sides were made by the women, but the painted designs upon these baskets were applied by the men, in line with their monopoly on all work that required paint. These baskets of various sizes but little variation in shape were used for all domestic tasks involving the collection, storing, transporting, and preparing of vegetable foods, and were sufficiently watertight to enable water also to be carried in them. Ordinary wooden spears (without barbs or painted designs) and a great variety of throwing sticks were made by all men, young or old, but important old men bothered with them very little, considering such routine manufacture beneath them. These workaday spears and throwing sticks lay around every camp in abundance, and a man who needed spears or sticks in a hurry could always gather up a bundle in a few minutes. Small boys picked up the techniques of making spears and throwing sticks by spending time with older boys who in turn improved their skill both in making and using hunting weapons by spending time with the local young men.

Although much of this learning was fairly random, other instruction was not. During his initiation period a youth spent long intervals isolated in the bush with a couple of older teachers from whom he received training in religious and ritual matters. At the same time, of course, it was inevitable that the novice absorb some of the older men's experience in bushcraft. There was no corresponding initiation period for girls. What they learned, they learned first from the older women of their childhood household and later from the older women of the husband's household into which they moved as child-brides after puberty. In all households the supervision by the elderly women of all younger women included the training of both female children and young wives in the things all females should know—things which were mostly concerned with collecting and preparing vegetable foods and the making of baskets.

In pre-white times Tiwi males wore no clothing whatever. The Mission insisted on calico loincloths, but, at least in the 1928-29 period, one could

---

[8] Female mourners were required to daub their bodies with white clay as a sign of mourning, but this paint was smeared haphazardly over their bodies and faces without any attempt at regularity or design, in contrast to the careful paint designs on the men's bodies.

observe the spontaneous gesture with which men, on leaving the Mission, automatically threw off their loincloths at the Mission fence and headed for the bush as naked as the day they were born. Women, in pre-white days, habitually carried a piece of bark which they held in front of themselves whenever they met a male. As soon as string or rope was introduced by the early white contacts, the women found it more convenient to tie some sort of band around their waists and double the piece of bark over this waistband. This was much handier since it left the hands free, but the bark, being stiff and unsecured, was at best a very capricious covering, and old women in the midst of public arguments often tore off their aprons and threw them at their opponents as a gesture of contempt.

Young women were more decorous and fussed modestly with their bark aprons when young men were present rather in the same way as American coeds fuss with their skirts in crowded classrooms. Theoretically, young women were supposed never to meet either young men or men outside their own household, and so the bark apron, carried in the hand, was in aboriginal times merely something to have in case of emergency. It was noticeable in Tiwi ceremonies that when the women danced, they did nothing with their hands. We think this was because, in pre-white days, their right hands, at least, were needed to hold their bark aprons in front of their pubic regions, since at dances they were in the presence of strange men.

This brief account of the daily and yearly life of the Tiwi households enables us to draw a few important conclusions about their economic life:

1. Compared with many of the mainland tribes, the Tiwi were economically rather well-off, in that the bigger household units were usually able to produce a food surplus.

2. This food surplus varied directly with the number of working wives that a household head possessed.

3. A household head with many wives was therefore, in Tiwi terms, a wealthy man who could retire entirely from the food quest and devote his time to other activities.

4. Such men were able to devote full time to other activities such as manufacturing useful and ceremonial objects and participation in ceremonial affairs and public life.

5. Wealthy men, active in one or all of these pursuits, were the "big men" of the tribe. In each band there were two or three such men, and in the whole tribe perhaps less than twenty had attained full success or were ranked by public opinion as being the most admired and influential. The next chapter examines the career patterns by which every male Tiwi sought to become, and a few succeeded in becoming, a big man.

3

The Prestige
and Influence System

To BECOME a really big man, or even a minor figure among the elders, a Tiwi had to devote all his adult life to that goal. Careers were built up and influential positions gained not by executing spectacular coups at any one time, but by slow, devious maneuvering and dealing in influence throughout adulthood. Men in their early thirties invested their very small assets in the hope of large returns twenty years later, and if the anthropologist witnessed the initial investment he was not around to witness the final return; or if he witnessed the return he found it difficult to reconstruct all the relevant details of the initial investment. A man in 1928 bestowed his daughter in a certain direction because of some deal back in 1900, arranged by men many of whom were now dead. And the bestowal in 1928 was done in such a way as to bind the hands of men negotiating in 1960, some of whom were infants in 1928.[1]

The Tiwi influence and career patterns can best be compared to a sort of nonstop bridge game wherein the scores were never totaled up nor a new game ever started on a clean slate.[2] Whenever an observer came in, he always

---

[1] A typical illustration of this situation arose during the writing of this book. In 1928-29 Hart had observed Padimo beginning to acquire a number of bestowed wives. Being interested in the status of Padimo twenty-five years later, he included Padimo in a list of inquiries to Pilling. Pilling's reply: "Re Padimo. I am almost certain that he was the 'Paddy' who died leaving several widows, in February, 1953, about three months before I got to the Islands. The natives did not like to talk much about him while I was there (because of the taboo on dead men's names) and his widows were still being fought over. The fights over his widows did not end until the week I left (if they really did then)." Thus the deals which Hart saw in 1928-29 were having delayed repercussions when Pilling was there in 1953-54.

[2] We use bridge rather than poker as our analogy because nobody ever "went broke" in Tiwi influence competition and nobody ever "won the pot," because there was no pot to win. The scoring was always, so to speak, on a comparative basis and everybody, even the most unsuccessful man, had some score relative to his competitors.

entered in the middle of the game and found the current hands being played with all the old scores back for at least two generations influencing the play of the present hands. The game never had a beginning or an end; every new player had to start in the middle and make the best of whatever assets he had by way of kinship, clanship, household membership, and help from older players. Similarly, any attempt to describe the operations involved or the "rules" of the game must perforce start in the middle.

The "game" was one of trying to win friends and increase prestige and influence over others. The "assets," in a tribe with such minimal material possessions as the Tiwi, were mostly intangible ones such as friendship, "help," goodwill, respect of others, control over others, importance, and influence. Even in our culture such things are difficult to express in concrete or tangible symbols. The most concrete symbol of Tiwi success was the possession of surplus food, for this not only permitted its possessor to make gifts to others and throw large parties for which he picked up the check, but also gave him lots of leisure time to devote to social and political life. Since a man required a large number of women in his work force if he was to build up a surplus of food, in the final analysis it was control of women that was the most tangible index of power and influence. Women were the main currency of the influence struggle, the main "trumps" in the endless bridge game.

It should be noticed that we stress the value of women as women rather than as wives or bestowable daughters. To a smart Tiwi politician, wives or daughters were assets but so was his mother—if submissive to her son's wishes. So were his sisters—if amenable. A bachelor at the age of thirty who had several sisters was a lucky young man, especially if those sisters already had daughters to their current husbands. As successful old men used their infant daughters to gain influence and buy satellites, so young men used their mothers and their sisters—if they could.

Thus the psychological line between the attitude of a man toward a wife and his attitude toward a sister or a daughter was a very thin one. A Tiwi elder had many women related to him in some way—as wives, as daughters, as step-daughters, as sisters, as sisters' daughters, as wards, and as mother—and all of these were part of his assets or capital. The fact that he had sexual rights to the wives and not to the daughters or the sisters was only of minor relevance. What was of major relevance was that they were all women whom he could use—or try to use—as investment funds in his own career of influence seeking. The devious details of Tiwi prestige and influence operations are much easier to follow if one keeps in mind the crucial fact that the Tiwi men valued women as political capital available for investment in gaining the goodwill of other men more than they were interested in them as sexual partners. Some of the more senile elders were quite vague about the young girls in their household; such an old man was sure only of the fact that a girl, by being in his household, was part of his capital. Which were his daughters and which were recently joined young wives was a question that had to be referred to the old wives who kept track of such academic details.

Women were, however, a form of capital that possessed the power of talking back to the investors. As daughters or as wives they were quite thoroughly subordinate to the wishes of their fathers or husbands, and Tiwi wives were as frequently and as brutally beaten by their husbands as wives in any other savage society. But as mothers and as sisters the women were not coerced by their sons and their brothers. On the contrary, sons or brothers wishing to use their mothers or their sisters in their political schemes (typically when those mothers or sisters became or were about to become widows) could only do so with the active collaboration of the women concerned. Tough-minded young widows could drive a hard bargain with their brothers as to where they remarried, since each needed the other to make the remarriage acceptable to the tribe at large and to beat down the other competitors (the dead husbands' brothers, for example) who wished to control the remarriage of the widows. Young girls thus had no bargaining power but young widows had a good deal. Old mothers with influential senior sons were extremely powerful. Any affront to an old woman was an affront to her sons, and some of the strongest influence networks were alliances of several senior brothers, in which their old mother seemed to be the mastermind and the senior sons largely the enforcers of what the old mother and her middle-aged daughters (their sisters) had decided among themselves.

Thus, for women, as for men, age and political skill were the crucial factors in determining their position. Young girls were chattels and as such were passed around from husband to husband. But with increasing age, smart young women, especially in alliance with their smart young brothers, could control their own fate with some firmness, and if they and their brothers had a shrewd old mother (also with powerful senior brothers still alive) to advise them and support them, then the decisions of such a group as to where the girls remarried were very difficult decisions for anybody else to combat or oppose. Not as independent operators, but as behind-the-scenes allies of their sons and brothers, Tiwi mothers and sisters enjoyed much more essential freedom in their own careers as often-remarried widows than would appear at first sight in a culture which ostensibly treated all women as currency in the political careers of the men. No matter how males, both old and young, might connive, they were constantly aware that no remarriage of a widow could ever be arranged and made to stick unless the widow herself was agreeable.

In the limited space available, all we can offer are a few samples of how the influence game was played by a few selected individuals of various ages. Age was of great importance in Tiwi careers and therefore we select our samples from all the adult male age-groups. We have selected them all from the same band—the Malauila—so as to show as clearly as possible the interplay between one career and another for men of the same band. And finally we select men of the Malauila band for our examples because in 1928-29 it was a band little affected as yet by the outside influences—Catholic missionaries and Japanese pearl divers—which were beginning to modify Tiwi marriage customs among some of the other bands.

The Beginning of Tiwi Careers

The Malauila in 1928-29 consisted of forty-nine males and sixty females of all ages. The males were divided into the following age groups:

20 years and below	28
between 21 and 30	7
between 31 and 42	7
between 43 and 55	4
over 55	3
Total	49

Of the twenty-eight males aged 20 or below, none had a wife of any kind, and none of them expected or were expected to have one. This group comprised the male children—boys and youths—and such males were of no importance whatever in the Tiwi scheme of things. They lived in the households of older men and were ignored by the male elders.

The next group, the seven men between 21 and 30, was the group of young men whom the elders were just beginning to take seriously. The younger of them were almost indistinguishable from the "youths," while the older of them were beginning to be watched by the seniors with some interest. Of the seven, six were neither married to a wife of any sort nor promised a wife. One, called Banana by the whites, was a man of about 28 and married to an ancient crone who was childless by three previous husbands, but she was in the category of "disputed" wife since her young husband had only been able to acquire and hold her because of abnormal circumstances arising from the presence of white buffalo-hunters on Melville Island some years previously. Under pre-white conditions, none of the seven men under 30 would have had a wife of any kind.

The years between 30 and 40 were the crucial years for Tiwi men in their establishment of households and careers. It was during this period that men normally married their first ancient widows and the "likely to be successful" became sorted out from the less-likely. As they passed into their thirties, men were allowed to enter for the first time into the influence game and, as the most junior players, they entered it by becoming subordinates and satellites of the bigger and more senior players, or by making alliances among themselves so as to pool their small individual assets.

In this age group in 1928-29, there were seven Malauila men ranging in age from around 31 to 42. One (Tiberun) was still unmarried and unpromised. He was thus (at age about 33) the oldest bachelor in the band. Not unnaturally he spent a good deal of time with other bands or at the Mission in the hope that his failure to get started in Malau might be remedied by elders of other bands or even by the priests. Tiberun was an older full brother of Banana, the 28-year-old married irregularly to a woman whom he had "stolen." A glance at their family tree revealed one potent reason why Tiberun was still a bachelor and why Banana had acted so impulsively and thereby gotten himself in the bad graces of the elders. The two men were the eldest of four brothers without any full sisters and as such they were necessarily handicapped in their career struggle. Elders seeking satellites or contemporaries seeking allies looked askance at men without sisters, for such men could have no sisters' daughters to use in the marriage-arrangements struggle. The mother of Tiberun and Banana was dead, but even were she still alive, few men would have been interested in marrying a widow whose only living children were sons. Widows without daughters and bachelors without sisters rated very low in the scale of desirable assets sought either by elders or by contemporaries.

Tiberun was thus the only bachelor in the 30-42 age group. Of the remainder we select Teapot as an example of another man who failed to get started. Teapot was at least 35, and about seven years previously he had "stolen" a wife from an elder. This wife was no ancient and shop-worn widow like the wife Banana had "stolen," but a young girl who had been betrothed in due form to an elder by her father. How Teapot had managed to get away with her is too complicated an incident to unravel here, and in any case it hadn't done Teapot much good. After presenting Teapot with a baby boy the young woman died, and Teapot, with a now six-year-old son, was more or less an outcast among the Malauila. No elder wanted him as a satellite and none of his contemporaries wanted him as an ally. His mother was dead and his only sister was married to a Munupula elder. This sister in Munupi was his only asset and one which a different man might have used as a means to better himself. But Teapot, instead of using this small asset to get started on a career, had chosen to defy the rules and "steal" an elder's bestowed wife. "Stealing" an old widow was reprehensible conduct in the eyes of the elders; stealing a young bestowed wife was unforgivable. Hence Teapot, since his crime, had received no bestowal, had been able to marry no widow, and was wanted by no one as an ally.

A complete contrast to these two unsuccessful men in their thirties was provided by the case of Gitjara, who was about the same age as Tiberun. Gitjara, it is true, had sisters, and that was always a help. Using his sisters (already married and bearing children to an elder) as bait, Gitjara when he was about 28 proposed an alliance to L. F. B., a rather feeble man about five years older than himself, who was not doing very well in the influence race. The gist of the proposal was that, since both their mothers were still alive and each married to an old man who could not last much longer, Gitjara should marry the ancient mother of L. F. B. when she became a widow, and L. F. B. should marry Gitjara's mother when that old lady became a widow. Perhaps the idea originated with the two old women rather than with either of the young men. Since such arrangements were essentially plots or schemes, it is impossible to determine who conceived them in the first place—old women ambitious to aid their sons or young men ready to use their mothers as long-term gambits to ultimately provide themselves with young wives. Mother-exchange operations were probably first conceived at high-level strategy conferences in which smart mothers and dull mothers, smart sons and dull sons were all present, and the final plan emerged from consensus.

In this case the former husbands of the two old women both died conveniently soon and within about three years of each other and, according to plan, there came into existence a household of two men in their thirties each married to the elderly mother of the other. Gitjara and L. F. B. thus set up jointly the foundations of their households and began their careers as a joint enterprise.

Gitjara had two sisters, both married to White Man, an elder, and already the mothers of daughters to him. By marrying Gitjara's mother, L. F. B. automatically became the nominal father of these women, and in the event of White Man's death would have, as such, some say in where they remarried. But the right of the step-father to redispose widowed step-daughters was always disputed by the brothers (or even sons) of the step-daughters, provided those brothers (or sons) were old enough or influential enough for their wishes to be taken seriously. Thus we may say that in putting L. F. B. into position as his own step-father, Gitjara's main object had been to get a satellite or henchman of his own into the position of step-father of his sisters (the wives of White Man) so that when they became widows there would be no conflict between the wishes of their brother and the wishes of their step-father as to whom they should remarry. L. F. B. as step-father was, so to speak, a stooge for Gitjara the brother.

Conversely, L. F. B. had two sisters both married to Ki-in-kumi, the most powerful elder in Malau. By marrying the mother of L. F. B., Gitjara became the step-father of two of Ki-in-kumi's wives, thus immediately (despite his youth) becoming technically the father-in-law of that powerful old man, and a man with some say in where those two wives of Ki-in-kumi would remarry on Ki-in-kumi's death. As step-father of such widows, Gitjara would have to make his wishes prevail as against the wishes of their brothers, but the only brother was L. F. B. and his vote was obviously in Gitjara's pocket.

By engineering this double shuffle of two elderly widows, each with daughters, Gitjara had launched his career as a marriage manipulator. Almost before it was concluded he became involved in another widow operation. We will omit the intricate details, but can say that he emerged from this with a second wife for himself, this one (naturally) also a widow but quite a young widow. This woman had already borne four sons and one daughter to her previous husband but was still young enough when Gitjara took her over in 1926 to bear him a son (her last) in 1927. In Tiwi terms the acquisition of this widow by Gitjara was a real achievement for the young man, not because of her comparative youth nor because of the son she bore him but because among the children by her previous marriage was a daughter aged about nine at the time she remarried Gitjara. To become the step-father of such a young girl was a real asset for the young operator. Her dead father had bestowed this child on Summit, another of the same Malauila age group of 30-year-olds and hence one of Gitjara's rivals and competitors in the influence struggle.

This created an intriguing situation since Summit, having had this child be-stowed on him at her birth some nine years previously, had thus acquired a bestowed wife at about age 27; Gitjara now 33 or so still had not received a bestowal. By remarrying the mother of Summit's young bestowed wife, Git-jara had turned the tables on one of his chief competitors among his age group. He could not, of course, alter the bestowal; in five or six years' time the girl would take up residence with Summit. But as the step-father who renamed the girl and the head of the household in which she would live for the next five years, Gitjara was in an excellent position to make Summit enter into a deal or two with him. He could drag his feet as to the time of the delivery of the girl to Summit; he could drop hints that there was something irregular about the bestowal to Summit in the first place, and so on; but whatever form of pressure he chose to exert on Summit, the latter well knew that all Gitjara wanted was to be cut in on some of Summit's deals and to be included in the network of Summit's alliances. The next move was now clearly up to Summit.

If Summit wished the nine-year-old girl now in Gitjara's household to be transferred promptly and without argument, he would be well advised to give some consideration to Gitjara, perhaps even the promise of one of his still-to-be-born daughters either as a wife or as a ward. Although not neces-sary, it would be a politically wise gesture. If he did so, both men would be gambling in futures. Since Summit's young wife was now nine years old, it would be at least six or seven years before she could produce a daughter (if at all) and another fourteen or fifteen years before any such daughter (if she lived) would be old enough to join Gitjara's household either as a wife or ward. Hence, under any such arrangement between the two young men, Summit would be giving something to Gitjara but in such a way that the latter could not collect for at least twenty years and might never collect.

Anthropologists will note that such arrangements still conformed to the patterns of cross-cousin marriage. Gitjara as *de jure* father delivers his "daughter" to Summit and thus becomes technically Summit's mother's brother or wife's father. Twenty years later (if all goes well) Summit delivers his daughter (by Gitjara's daughter) to Gitjara, thus becoming technically the mother's brother or wife's father of Gitjara. Gitjara himself might marry this daughter of Summit by his own step-daughter or treat her as a ward given to him by Summit and bestow her on some other man selected by himself; in the latter case he would be acting as father to his step-daughter's daughter. There were no clan barriers to such an arrangement, since fathers had to belong to clans different from those of their wives and of their daughters, step-daughters and daughters' daughters.

There were, of course, alternative actions or "deals" open to Summit and also to Gitjara, depending upon their plans in other directions. The pattern described above, however, was extremely common in Tiwi marriage arrangements, and often it was the reason why some very old man would receive some female infant as a wife: an agreement of this type had been made twenty or thirty years before, when the now senile old man was in his thirties and when the mother of the baby he was now receiving was married to some man long since dead. The circumstances were certainly right for such an arrangement in the Gitjara-Summit case of 1928.

If we now pause and look at the marriage career of Gitjara at the point it had reached by the time he was 33, we can separate out three distinct types of operation in which this admirable young man had engaged. His first marriage, with L. F. B.'s elderly mother, had brought into existence a joint household of young men and elderly widows which not only was a very satisfactory housekeeping arrangement but also put Gitjara and his ally, L. F. B., in a position to exert some influence on all the subsequent remarriages of their respective sisters.

Gitjara's marriage a few years later to a second widow put him in a position to enter into marriage arrangements even more directly, since the second widow had a daughter promised to Summit but still too young to take up residence with him. By dragging his feet on the fulfilment of this promise, Gitjara could put pressure on Summit and extract from the latter some sort of consideration to facilitate the delivery of the girl. Gitjara was thus well in the marriage-broker business before he had any children of his own and indeed before he had received any bestowal. This was the second type of operation for an up-and-coming young man, and it was one wherein a shrewd and aggressive operator would use the daughters of other men (that is, of a widow's previous husbands) in such a way as to attach all sorts of codicils and contingent interests and second mortgages to the original bestowal of those daughters, many of these collectable in full only in the far distant future, after all prior interests had been satisfied or had lapsed.

The third type of operation engaged in by Gitjara was, of course, to try and attract bestowed wives of his own. His vigorous operations, by age 33, in the widow remarriage field, were not only ends in themselves but also were the type of operation that attracted the approval of older men with daughters to bestow. Hence it is not surprising to find that by 1929 Gitjara, married to the two widows already mentioned, had received two bestowals. The older of these was a girl of ten rebestowed on Gitjara in 1927 when the man died upon whom she had been bestowed at birth. The second was a baby born in 1927 whose father was Tomitari of the Rangwila. (The choice of Gitjara as a son-in-law by Tomitari was so interesting that we shall discuss it later in this chapter.) Both these bestowals were made *after* Gitjara had engineered his remarriage of the two widows and as far as kinship was concerned had no connection whatever with these widows or their close relatives. We conclude, therefore, that widow remarriage could be used by alert and aggressive men in their early thirties for three purposes: (1) to establish households and obtain elderly housekeepers; (2) to establish low-priority rights in the daughters of the widows' previous husbands; and (3) to attract attention to themselves as smart operators and gain the attention and approval of older men. As an outgrowth of the third purpose, they were likely to attract bestowals. Hence we may say that among the Tiwi the best road to obtaining a young wife or several young wives was for a young man to be first successful in the manipulation of the remarriages of elderly widows, who were always in large supply. If a man showed skill and know-how in his early thirties among the widows, then in his late thirties and early forties young wives would be bestowed upon him in abundance. Such a lesson could not have a better exemplar than Gitjara. By age 33 he had done so well among the widows that his first *young* wife would be joining his household by the time he was thirty-eight or thirty-nine, and another was already a year old. Clearly he was a young man of promise and one to be watched—and cultivated.

Summit, a man slightly older than Gitjara, must be dealt with very briefly, since the reasons for his success would take us too far afield. In 1929 he had a list of six wives, the only resident one being an elderly widow. The other five were bestowals and the eldest of these was the girl of ten whom we have already mentioned as being in the household of her step-father, Gitjara. Two more, younger than the ten-year-old, were in the household of Padimo (see below) and the remaining two were in the household of one of the elders of the Rangwila band. Summit, in Tiwi reckoning, was a Rangwila himself and had only moved to Malau a few years before. Some four years previously he had been a young Rangwila with no less than five bestowed child-wives. Three of these had been given him by an elder in Malau, two by an elder of his own band. The Malauila girls were older than the two Rangwila girls and his Malauila father-in-law was older than his Rangwila father-in-law. Summit therefore moved north to supervise personally his interests in Malau. He had, however, been out-maneuvered when the Malauila father-in-law died, since Gitjara had then been able to remarry the mother of Summit's eldest child-wife and Padimo had been able to remarry the mother of the other two little girls. Having thus moved to Malau to be near to and a satellite of his elderly Malauila father-in-law, Summit now found himself the technical son-in-law of two young men of his own age group who were among his keen competitors in the influence struggle. To ensure that his three promised Malauila child-wives joined his household when old enough, he now needed to make some arrangements with Gitjara and Padimo. Summit had gotten his bestowals rather early and rather easily but he still had the problem of nailing them down.

While thus engaged in acquiring five bestowed young wives and trying to promote their safe delivery when ready, Summit had married a widow not much more than forty years old but childless by her two previous husbands.[3] Such a widow at least provided him with a food-getter and housekeeper and enabled him to establish a household into which his five bestowed wives would enter as they successively reached the proper age. Thus Summit's household in 1929 consisted only of himself and his *palimaringa* wife. Within the next fifteen years it would be increased by the addition of at least five young wives,

---

[3] Such women who had reached middle age without surviving children were called by a special term, *palimaringa,* in Tiwi and the term referred to childlessness rather than barrenness. Summit's widow, for example, had borne two children, both of whom had died in infancy, and she was classified as a *palimaringa*. When a *palimaringa* became very, very old indeed, the word changed to *timaringa*.

plus any new bestowals, plus any further widows Summit might find it to his interest (and power) to remarry.

Padimo, who thus enters our story as one of Summit's rivals and one of his nominal fathers-in-law, was also a Rangwila who had moved to Malau at the call of an elderly father-in-law. He presents another pattern of Tiwi upward mobility and one that was statistically more frequent than the rather tortuous road followed by men like Gitjara. Padimo had been chosen as a nephew worth supporting by old Ki-in-kumi, the wealthiest of the Malauila. The earliest proof of Ki-in-kumi's patronage of Padimo had come in 1925-26 when an old man died, leaving eight widows of very diverse ages. Three of these "widows," aged respectively 17, 13, and 9 at the time of the death of their first husband, were daughters of Ki-in-kumi. Being so young and their brothers being equally young, their father's right to arrange their remarriage was unchallenged and Ki-in-kumi reassigned[4] them as wives to young Padimo, then aged about thirty-three. The eldest of the three girls had already borne two female children to the dead man, these being the two girl babies mentioned above as having been promised to Summit.

As well as the three young widows, Padimo had also obtained at the same redistribution the oldest and most haggish of the dead man's eight wives. It was at the same redistribution that Gitjara had obtained his second widow (the mother of the girl promised to Summit). Thus through Ki-in-kumi's influence, Padimo had obtained four "widows" of the eight left by the man who died in 1925-26; Gitjara, working without a powerful patron, had been lucky to obtain one.

Ki-in-kumi had subsequently followed up this initial selection of Padimo as a favored sister's son by giving further daughters to him as they were born. Consequently, by 1929 Padimo's wife list consisted of the following:

A. One extremely ancient widow.
B. One wife aged about 20, daughter of Ki-in-kumi, mother already of two daughters by a previous husband who, before his death, bestowed these daughters on Summit.
C. One wife aged about 17, daughter of Ki-in-kumi; had just had her first child (who lived only a week); had previously been bestowed on the dead husband of wife B, but was too young to join his household before he died.
D. Three more girls, daughters of Ki-in-kumi, the eldest about 12 and hence old enough to have been bestowed on the same previous husband as wives B and C; the other two aged 2 and 1 and hence born since his death. All three of these were still resident in their father's household.

---

[4] It is difficult to decide whether such reassignments of female children by their father, on the death of the man to whom he had first betrothed them, should be called "rebestowals" or "remarriages." We prefer the first word since such "child-widows" were usually reassigned by their fathers (if still alive) without any challenge to his rights to do so. They therefore do not differ from original bestowals at birth except for the awkward semantic fact that the man to whom such a "child-wife" was reassigned was technically her second husband.

With a lineup such as this by the time he was thirty-six, Padimo was clearly in process of going places in Tiwi society. The only weakness one could see in his position was that it all derived from the favor of one patron, and no old man with daughters, other than Ki-in-kumi, had seen fit to bestow a girl upon him. It should be noted that in 1929, though Padimo had two young wives resident in his household, he still had no children of his own. His first child, born that year, lived only a few days. The only children in residence were the two girls promised to Summit by the previous husband of their mother. Their bestowal on Summit was a matter beyond Padimo's control though he could use them to force some concessions from Summit just as Gitjara could with the girl in his household. But as Padimo's young wives began to bear daughters of his own, his bestowal of them would be less encumbered by the commitments of any predecessor. While Ki-in-kumi lived, Padimo would have to consider his obligations to that old man and at least consult with Ki-in-kumi as to how he should bestow his female children, since any such children would be the daughters' daughters of the old man. Nor would the death of Ki-in-kumi leave Padimo entirely free to bestow his own daughters anywhere he wished. Many of the girls already given to him as wives by Ki-in-kumi had mothers who possibly, and brothers who certainly, would outlive Ki-in-kumi. On the old man's death, all of his numerous wives would remarry—some of the older ones probably to ambitious younger men—and these new husbands of the widows of Ki-in-kumi would begin interfering with and trying to alter the arrangements made for his daughters by the old man during his lifetime. Thus Padimo would find himself stuck with a group of new and antagonistic fathers-in-law in place of the old, indulgent father-in-law who had been responsible for his success so far. Padimo's problem was basically how to hold, after Ki-in-kumi's death, the favored position he had gained during the old man's lifetime through the old man's favor.

In the meantime, with Ki-in-kumi still alive and powerful, Padimo had the biggest and fastest expanding household among the Malauila men in their thirties. The only remaining man in this age group was Boya who was the oldest of them all, being at least 42 years old in 1928. As might be expected, his career illustrates some new facets of the Tiwi influence struggle.

Structurally the position of Boya was simple but politically it was complex. His father had been a henchman and satellite of Ki-in-kumi in the early career of that old operator and roughly had had somewhat the same relationship to the young Ki-in-kumi as L. F. B. had to Gitjara. Boya's father, the satellite, left only two widows (an indication of his mediocrity) and these two widows had been remarried by Ki-in-kumi, the patron. One of these widows was Boya's mother, and Boya was too young at the time to have any say in where his mother remarried. Ki-in-kumi's interest in marrying Boya's mother was not of course because he thus acquired Boya as a step-son, but because he acquired Boya's sisters as step-daughters. Step-sons were liabilities which new husbands had to take over in order to get rights in the real assets —the step-daughters.

Some years later, when Boya had reached a reasonable age like 30, Ki-in-kumi had arranged for him to marry a very ancient and childless widow (*palimaringa*) more than twenty years older than himself. This was all that Ki-in-kumi considered he needed to do for his step-son, and in Tiwi terms it was almost a gesture of contempt and an open indication that Ki-in-kumi, by providing him with an old woman who was childless but could cook, was not interested in helping Boya toward a career. Since the joining up of Boya to the crone took place shortly after the death of Boya's mother, who had lived with her sons in Ki-in-kumi's household, Ki-in-kumi by producing the old widow for Boya was telling him in effect to get out and start his own household now that his mother was dead.

In 1928 we found Boya aged about 42 married to the crone of 65. But he, she, and Boya's younger brother of 24 were still living in Ki-in-kumi's household. Ki-in-kumi's detestation of him was notorious and yet Boya had by now no less than four young bestowed child-wives growing up elsewhere. No one of these bestowals had come from Malau but were bestowals from different fathers of baby girls in other bands. At first sight this presented a curious situation. Within his own band Boya appeared a complete failure, suffering so severely from Ki-in-kumi's hostility that he had received no bestowals and at age 42 did not even have a separate household of his own. But how could this judgment be squared with the four bestowals from elders of other bands? Clearly none of the causes of success so far analyzed fitted the case of Boya.

Further research into who lived with whom as distinct from who was married to whom revealed that not only was "the household" of Boya, his elderly wife, and his younger brother an integral part of the Ki-in-kumi "establishment," but also that Padimo with his "household" was part of that establishment. Padimo, like Boya, had one elderly wife but he also had five bestowed wives, all daughters of Ki-in-kumi. We said above that the two eldest of these five girls being now aged 20 and 17 respectively were in residence with their husband, while the three youngest, not having reached puberty, were still "with their father." Actual observation showed that this was an academic distinction, since the households of Padimo, the son-in-law, and Ki-in-kumi, the father-in-law, were parts of the same establishment. When one of Ki-in-kumi's daughters bestowed on Padimo became old enough to "leave her father and join her husband," she did not have to move her residence or even change her daily work routines. She merely sat at night around the campfire of her older sisters (Padimo's wives) instead of around the campfire of her younger sisters (Ki-in-kumi's daughters). She remained part of the same establishment.

Padimo, it will be remembered, was the young man whom Ki-in-kumi had attracted from Rangu to Malau by liberally bestowing him with child-wives. Padimo had thus moved into the northern band and by 1928 had moved right into Ki-in-kumi's camp, where he functioned as a sort of executive officer and heir apparent to the old man. In the same camp, though in a very different capacity, was Boya, the 42-year-old despised step-son. Many roads thus led to Ki-in-kumi's household, but before discussing the large establishment of that wealthy elder, we will first summarize, in Table I, the marital conditions of the eight young men we have been discussing.

TABLE I

THE MALAUILA YOUNG MEN IN 1928-29

Name	Age	Resident Old Wives (Ex-widows)	Resident Young Wives (Bestowals)	Promised Wives (Under 14)	Own Children
Tiberun	33	0	0	0	0
Banana	28	1	0	0	0
Teapot	35	0[a]	0	0	1
Gitjara	33	2	0	2	1
L. F. B.	38	1	0	1	0
Summit	36	1	0	5	0
Padimo	36	1	2	3	0[b]
Boya	42	1	0	4	0

[a] Teapot's "stolen" wife was dead.
[b] Padimo's first child, born in 1929, lived only a few days.

This table presents a summary of many of our earlier attempts at generalization. The only Malauila under the age of 43 who had a bestowed young wife old enough to live with him was Padimo, who was thus exceptionally lucky. Leaving out young Banana, five of the seven men between the ages of 30 and 42 had young females promised to them, but these were mostly babies or children who would not come into residence for several years. Six of the seven had married widows, mostly elderly widows, well in advance of the arrival of young wives and before any father had bestowed a daughter on them. Finally, and a point not made before, men of this age group rarely had any children of their own. The only entries in the last column of Table I are the irregularly born son of Teapot; Padimo's first daughter who died virtually at birth; and the 1-year-old son of Gitjara who was the last child born to his second ex-widow. Tiwi men rarely had young wives until they were around forty; they even more rarely had any children of their own before that age. Padimo's dead baby and Gitjara's 1-year-old son were exceptional; the zeros in the last column against the names of Boya (42), L. F. B. (38), and Summit (36) represent the normal situation for Tiwi men of such ages.

In terms of success (as measured by bestowals) Padimo and Summit (largely through the patronage of elders) and Boya and Gitjara (largely through their own operations) were the coming young men among the Malauila. Of the others, L. F. B. was approaching forty with few assets and no influence, and the other three, Tiberun, Banana, and Teapot, had not even got started in the influence race.

A Very Successful Elder: Ki-in-kumi

The most influential man in Malau and the head of the biggest household was Ki-in-kumi. Since he had been born around 1863-64 and had been a "young operator" somewhat before 1900, the deals by which he got his career launched were difficult to reconstruct. The results of them, plus the fact that he lived long enough to draw full dividends from them, gave him by 1928-29 a wife-list of twenty-one. These had been accumulated as follows:

> When around 30 years old he remarried two elderly widows and a year or two later received his first bestowal. Thus by age 33 he had three wives. On that foundation he went ahead thus:
>
> | | | *Total* |
> |---|---|---|
> | *At age 33* | | |
> | Had two widows and one bestowed wife | | 3 |
> | *Between age 33 and age 43* | | |
> | Remarried two more widows and had three more bestowed wives join him | +5 | 8 |
> | *Between age 43 and age 53* | | |
> | Three more bestowed wives came into residence | +3 | 11 |
> | (During these twenty years at least five bestowed wives died in infancy or childhood) | +5 | 16 |
> | *Between age 53 and age 65* | | |
> | Two more bestowed wives joined him and he married 2 more widows (one the mother of Boya) | +4 | 20 |
> | Now at age 66 there is still one more bestowed wife, aged about 9, in her father's household | +1 | 21 |

Thus his list of twenty-one wives was made up of six elderly widows and fifteen bestowed or rebestowed young wives.

By 1928-29 five of his bestowed wives had died before puberty and one was still with her father. Three of his six widows were dead. Subtracting these nine women, we find that his current household contained twelve resident and active wives: the oldest about sixty, two in their fifties, four in their forties or thirties, three in their twenties, and the two youngest around seventeen or eighteen years of age. Almost all of them had borne children since joining his household, but the death rate had been high among Ki-in-kumi's children and from all of his wives he had only eight living children of whom six were girls. Five of these six daughters he had bestowed or rebestowed on Padimo (see above) and the sixth on a middle-aged Rangwila. His oldest living daughter was the girl of 20 married to Padimo. His oldest living son was a boy of 18, despite the fact that Ki-in-kumi had been "a married man" for over thirty-five years. This was a situation which many Tiwi elders found themselves in at the close of long and successful lives. With numerous wives, numerous step-sons, large households to be managed, and large estates to be liquidated after their deaths, their oldest real sons (as distinct from step-sons) were still boys or youths and as such quite unsuitable as executive assistants while the old man lived or as heirs or executors after the old man died. Quite apart from kinship considerations, the Tiwi emphasis on age and seniority made it impossible for Ki-in-kumi to utilize in any capacity his 18-year-old son. A youth of that age was a nonentity, whoever his father.

TABLE II
KI-IN-KUMI'S ESTABLISHMENT

(Ages in brackets)		Males	Females
Head (Ki-in-kumi	66)	1	0
Oldest step-son (Boya	42)	1	0
Sister's son (Padimo	36)	1	0
Old wives (of all three adult men)		0	5
Young wives (including Padimo's 2)		0	11
Young males (sons and step-sons)		8	0
Young females (daughters and step-daughters)		0	5
Totals		11	21

Confronted by this situation, Ki-in-kumi in his advancing years had summoned Padimo, a sister's son in his early thirties, to come from Rangu and become his chief lieutenant. The youth of his own son had been a factor in his selection of Padimo. The presence in his camp of an older step-son, Boya, had been another factor. Boya, the step-son, was more than twenty years older than the son, and at least six years older than Padimo, the chosen instrument. Padimo, as we have seen, moved right in, fused his own small household with Ki-in-kumi's large one, and became Ki-in-kumi's Man Friday. Boya, the step-son, though married to a widow, refused to move out. Thus, among other things, we have to distinguish between Ki-in-kumi's household of twelve resident wives enumerated above, and Ki-in-kumi's establishment which contained Padimo, Boya, and the various people attached by marriage or kinship to them. Padimo had an old wife and two young wives (daughters of Ki-in-kumi). Boya had an old wife and a younger brother. There were a number of younger step-children of both sexes also resident with Ki-in-kumi. The full size and make-up of his establishment is given in Table II.

The Establishments of Malau

There were, besides Ki-in-kumi, six other elders of the Malauila band. Two of these, the brothers Enquirio and Merapanui, were well over sixty and deserve, both by age and by success, to be labeled senior elders. The remaining four ranged in age from about 45 to nearly 60 and since none of them were particularly successful we call them the junior elders. In Table III we have listed the seven "establishments" in which lived all the members of the band. We mean by an establishment a food-production and food-consumption unit. Ki-in-kumi's establishment contained three married men—himself, Boya, and Padimo—and therefore contained three households. Economically it was one establishment, since the sixteen wives it contained worked as a team and the food they produced was consumed by the thirty-two total members of the establishment. For comparative purposes in Table III we list Ki-in-kumi's establishment as Unit I and give the personnel breakdown of the other six establishments that made up the total population of Malau. Unit II is the joint enterprise maintained by the other two senior elders, the brothers Enquirio and Merapanui. To this we have added the pathetic and ostracized Teapot and his motherless son, since when they ate at all they ate as hangers-on of the Enquirio-Merapanui menage. Unit III is the establishment jointly maintained by the brothers White Man and Ku-nai-u-ua. Since the oldest wife of Ku-nai-u-ua was Summit's mother, that young man, together with the elderly ex-widow who was so far his only resident wife, lived in this establishment. Units IV and V present no difficulty; they are the small households of the other two junior elders Pingirimini and Tipiperna-gerai respectively. Unit VI is the joint enterprise of Gitjara and L. F. B., containing largely old ladies and young men. Unit VII is the remarkable menage that had gathered round the elderly widow whom young Banana had illegally "married." To this couple

TABLE III

THE FOOD PRODUCTION UNITS OF MALAU

Unit	Married Males	Unmarried Males[a]	Old Wives[b]	Young Wives	Girls Under 14	Total Persons
I	3	8	5	11	5	32
II	3	9	1	7	11	31
III	3	2	2	3	5	15
IV	1	5	0	1	1	8
V	1	2	0	1	2	6
VI	2	5	3	0	1	11
VII	1?	4	1	0	0	6
Total	14	35	12	23	25	109

a Unmarried males include all males from male infants to men around 30, or more.
b The division between old wives and young wives is arbitrary. Several of the young wives were 40, others only 14 or 15.
? The question mark in Unit VII refers to the difficulty of deciding whether Banana should be classified as married.

had attached themselves Tiberun (Banana's unmarried older brother), two younger brothers, and another male orphan who had apparently moved in for want of some better place to eat. The Banana menage thus had somewhat the appearance of a case of economic polyandry and somewhat the look of a fraternity house with an elderly housemother in residence. We include it as Unit VII since by so doing we are able to include in Table III all the hundred and nine people who made up the Malauila band in 1928-29 and allocate all of them to the economic units in which they functioned as food producers and food consumers.

The data in Table III merit close study. These seven establishments illustrate in capsule form several of the more significant emphases in Tiwi career patterns; indeed each might be said to illustrate some time point in the life careers of adult men and/or some degree of success or lack of success in becoming an influential man.

The Politics of Widow Remarriage

Ki-in-kumi's large establishment was the sort of set-up that every Tiwi sought to achieve but few accomplished. An establishment such as his meant wealth, power, prestige, and influence for its head, and, in Malau, Ki-in-kumi was the only man with such a household. With eleven males, many of them food producing; sixteen women, all of them food producing; and several of the girls under fourteen able to assist the older women, the amount of food this unit could collect in a day provided an ample food surplus for the establishment. A man whose household was a surplus food producer was a successful man. Moreover, since the large work force that produced the food surplus contained numerous young wives who (usually) could be relied upon also to produce numerous female babies, he was doubly blessed with both the requisites—surplus food and surplus daughters—necessary to increase his influence and make more people beholden to him or dependent on him. Of the thirty-five married women in Malau, sixteen, or over 45 percent, were in this one establishment.

By comparison, the other old men of Malau were less successful.[5] Through pooling their work forces, Enquirio and Merapanui had achieved an establishment (Unit II) almost as big as that of Ki-in-kumi, and probably its members ate almost as well as the members of his, but their effort was a shared effort and their influence and prestige had to be divided between them. They had been lucky with daughters but, divided between the two fathers, the eleven daughters in their establishment were less impressive than Ki-in-kumi's eight, and the total of seven young wives between them was quite overshadowed by Ki-in-kumi's nine. The two old brothers were successful men and headed a successful operation, but their prestige and success must be rated at least one whole degree below that of Ki-in-kumi.

Another pair of elderly brothers, White Man and Ku-nai-u-ua, had also joined forces (Unit III), but the results can be judged as only fair. They were at least the best off of their age group, the 45- to 55-year-olds, but the competition in that age group was weak, as can be seen by comparison of their establishment with Units IV and V, the households of Pingirimini and Tipiperna-gerai. Perhaps the best indication of the respective success in life of the seven oldest men is that given in the column of Table III headed "young wives." Of the twenty-three such women in the band, eighteen were in the establishments[6] of the three oldest men (Units I and II); the next five men in age shared the remaining five (Units III, IV, and V).

It might be thought that the small establishments of the unsuccessful junior elders like White Man, Ku-nai-u-ua, Pingirimini, and Tipiperna-gerai could be expected to increase sharply in size and these men to grow in relative prestige and influence when death removed the three old men at the heads

---

[5] It will be noticed that as we move into the older group of men we have to use their native names, since most of them had no "whiteman" names.

[6] Two of these eighteen were of course actually married to Padimo, but still part of the establishment of their father, Ki-in-kumi, since Padimo's wives all lived with Ki-in-kumi's wives.

of Units I and II and made their wives available for redistribution. The working of the Tiwi system made this possibility unlikely. Unsuccessful junior elders could not expect to step into the shoes of successful senior elders merely by outliving them; nor could one rise to power in the gerontocratic system merely by living past fifty-five. What was necessary was age *plus* ability, and the time to demonstrate the ability was in one's thirties. If it was not demonstrated and recognized by then, a man could not forge ahead in his middle forties and early fifties, for by then it was too late. This fact gave a certain cyclical quality to the transfer of influence in Tiwi. The influence of successful senior elders, to the extent that such an intangible thing was transferable at all, tended to skip a decade and bypass the men currently in the junior elder category in favor of the men in the current "young operator" category. Since Ki-in-kumi was already quite old, there was in 1929 a great deal of political maneuvering going on in Malau and elsewhere in anticipation of his death, and it was clear that the people most likely to profit by his death and the redistribution of his twelve resident wives (one-third of all resident wives in the band) were the men aged from thirty-two to forty-two such as Padimo, Boya, Summit, and Gitjara, all of whom were jockeying for position to take advantage of the death of any old man, especially such a wealthy elder as Ki-in-kumi. Some of the widows would undoubtedly remarry into other bands, but these younger Malauila, living with or near the old man's establishment, were already taking advantage of their strategic location to make some preliminary deals and marriage arrangements for the old man's widows even before his death. Neither Padimo, as Ki-in-kumi's son-in-law, nor Boya, as his nominal "son," could themselves marry any of the widows, but as resident members of his establishment and the only two men so situated, each was in an excellent spot to act as an honest broker in the disposal of Ki-in-kumi's large estate. Anybody interested in obtaining a widow or two at the death of Ki-in-kumi was well advised to have a few quiet words with either Padimo or Boya well ahead of time. Both of them had wives who lived and worked every day alongside Ki-in-kumi's womenfolk and thus they each had ideal communication systems to the women's side of the band. This was why they had held off setting up their own separate establishments though they were both married men. Neither were "heirs" of Ki-in-kumi in any strict Western use of that word, but it was obvious that it was their careers that would be promoted and their spheres of influence that would be enhanced by the death of Ki-in-kumi. The junior elders, all approaching or past the age of fifty with only small establishments and small spheres of influence, were being bypassed in the transfer of the old man's assets.

Every Tiwi anxious to obtain a Ki-in-kumi widow recognized the strategic positions of Padimo and Boya; the problem was to decide which broker to retain, since the positions of the two men in relation to Ki-in-kumi were so different. For the past four or five years Padimo had been the right-hand man and trusted lieutenant and undoubtedly it was he upon whom Ki-in-kumi was relying to carry out his own wishes about the distribution of his widows. We said earlier that old men found it difficult to control the remarriage of their widows with the same unchallenged authority with which they bestowed their daughters. Nevertheless they tried hard in many cases to do so. Ki-in-kumi was one who tried hard to make the decisions for his widows, by selecting Padimo as his trusted executor. If Padimo faithfully carried out the old man's wishes after he died, then the widows were not likely to come on the open market; they would be redistributed in accordance with the terms of Ki-in-kumi's will (in both senses of the word "will").

Though, of course, Padimo might prove to be a dishonest executor of the estate, there was a safeguard provided in that the new husbands whom Ki-in-kumi had selected for his wives were all aware of his wishes and hence if Padimo tried to depart from those wishes the cheated heirs would bring charges of double dealing and broken promises against him. But regardless of Padimo's honesty after the death, his position as Ki-in-kumi's trusted lieutenant clearly made him an unsuitable agent before the death for those numerous men who wanted some of Ki-in-kumi's future widows and who had not seen any indication that Ki-in-kumi had included them among his beneficiaries. The obvious young man for such men to use as their go-between and agent was Boya. Ki-in-kumi was hostile to him and had given him nothing willingly. Boya's presence in the old man's establishment was based on the nominal tie of Ki-in-kumi being the last husband of his mother to rename him before she died. Viewed thus, the two young men in Ki-in-kumi's household can be said to have become agents for two different networks of intrigue. Padimo was the manager and agent for all the men, including Ki-in-kumi himself, who wanted to perpetuate and continue the existing alliances and arrangements that Ki-in-kumi had built or helped to build during his long and successful career; Boya was the natural agent for all the men who, being outside that set of alliances, had nothing to gain from Ki-in-kumi's death unless his death dissolved the network of alliances and arrangements of which Ki-in-kumi had been the main architect. Padimo's responsibility was necessarily a sort of holding-together and preserving operation as the executor of an existing estate; Boya's clients were men hoping for fragmentation and subdivision not only of Ki-in-kumi's widows but also of the alliances and deals of which the widows were a part.

It is incidentally amusing, and also indicative of how the ever-present kinship ties affected all such deals and redeals, to note that if some of Boya's clients succeeded in grabbing off some of Ki-in-kumi's widows—despite the opposition, before his death, of Ki-in-kumi and the presumed opposition, after the death, of Padimo the executor—they were very liable thus to become automatically fathers-in-law of Padimo, since several of Ki-in-kumi's wives already had daughters who were bestowed on Padimo.

The question then of which agent was employed by the numerous men yearning to acquire one or more of Ki-in-kumi's widows was fairly well settled by the respective roles which the two young men occupied in the household. Men already well inside the Ki-in-kumi-centered alliances were relying on Padimo; men outside those alliances were relying on Boya to engineer a fluid situation and a more open market. In choosing an agent in this as in any other "deal," there was also the question of fee. Neither Padimo nor Boya would become involved or make any soundings among the widows unless there was something in it for them. Hence the client had to find out whether a promise of general goodwill and friendship was all that Boya (or Padimo) would ask in return for his services or whether the price would be much higher—perhaps as high as the bestowal of the client's next baby daughter. It was in such ways that widow-remarriage arrangements and infant bestowals were intertwined; a much-delayed bestowal to an apparently unrelated individual would be the ultimate pay-off to the broker or agent who had engineered a widow remarriage for the bestower years before.

This role of agent in the disposal of a dead man's widows was a type of operation best suited to men in the first stages of their own married lives —that is, to men in their middle thirties or very early forties who had perhaps married their first or second widows and who had as yet no young wives of their own in residence. Having no young wives to guard, they were able to get around easily on diplomatic missions and they had their own listening posts inside the world of women in the person of their own mothers (if still alive) and in the elderly widows whom they themselves had married. The ambitious young brokers were tipped off by their mothers and elderly wives as to how the young wives wished to be distributed and what the competing young brokers were trying to arrange. Thus when a wealthy old man like Ki-in-kumi died, the redistribution of his wives through remarriage was a matter that had been decided beforehand by an extraordinary complex tangle of semisecret arrangements and deals and promises, but the people most influential in arranging the redistribution were the young brokers who usually got few, if any, of the young widows for themselves but who collected their rewards in reputation, influence, alliances, and future bestowals from the men for whom they had acted as agents.

Thus the death of Ki-in-kumi or of any other old man with many wives tended to disperse the wives all over the tribe, with only one or two, or at most three, going to any one new husband. A large estate was almost always fragmented by the death of the old man who had built it up, and any one of his contemporaries was able to take over only a very small fraction of it at best. The levirate and sororate principles, though present, worked very feebly. The men who benefited most—not immediately, but eventually—were the young operators.[7] In such a manner Padimo and Boya were sure to be the long-term beneficiaries of Ki-in-kumi's death though neither of them could remarry any of his widows. The real heirs of the wealthy old men of sixty and over were the young men who happened to be between thirty-two and forty-two when those old men got near to death. The men between forty-five and fifty-five whose brokerage business ten years earlier had not been very skillfully

---

[7] At least some of the so-called "stolen" or disputed wives were widows who had insisted on marrying the younger agent instead of the older client, which put the young broker in the embarrassing position of saying to his client, "I cannot make delivery of the widow I acquired on your account; she insists on marrying me instead." Such an incident did not do his agency business much good but tended rather to frighten off clients.

handled, or who happened to be at the brokering age when no big households were being liquidated, found themselves in the position that Pingirimini and Tipiperna-gerai occupied in 1928-29. We know they had not been successful dealers in their thirties because we found them around the age of fifty with only one resident wife each and relatively few bestowals in prospect. Their earlier dealings in widows had not laid the right foundations for successful careers as elders. Even before he was forty, Padimo had five or six bestowed wives either in residence or in prospect, and Boya, not much over forty, had several already promised. The death of Ki-in-kumi in the near future would bring both of them more reputation and ultimately more bestowals in return for their skill (if they showed it) in the disposition of the estate. The inferiority of Pingirimini and Tipiperna-gerai to these younger men in the marriage and influence struggle was already apparent and would be even more accentuated by Ki-in-kumi's death.

The Politics of Bestowal

The above discussion of how younger men were indirectly benefited by the deaths or impending deaths of wealthy older men does not pretend to give an exhaustive list of all the considerations that went into the reallocation of a dead man's widows. We built our analysis around those factors which were paramount in the case of Ki-in-kumi's household. Other cases were different to the extent that there were real adult sons involved in them rather than a nominal "son" like Boya, or because in them the old man had not chosen a clear-cut executor as Ki-in-kumi had chosen Padimo, or because an old man had surviving brothers close to him in age and alliance who would emphasize the levirate principle and seek to have it followed in the relocation of their dead brother's widows. The few points we are seeking to emphasize among the many that might be emphasized in any exhaustive treatment of Tiwi widow remarriage are: 1) that widow remarriage was a very flexible area in which the ultimate disposition of the widows was decided by the manipulations and wishes of a wide range of individuals including both relatives and nonrelatives. The dead man himself; the fathers of the wives, if still alive; the brothers of the widows, if adults; the widows themselves, if strong minded; the executors of the dead man, if clearly nominated; and the numerous dealers and brokers on behalf of remote clients or even on their own account—all tried to make their own wishes prevail. The result was that no two cases were ever alike, but on balance 2) it was younger men rather than older men who were most likely to enhance their reputations and increase their assets in the long run as the results of these widow redeals, even though in the short run it was the older men who remarried most of the widows, especially the younger widows.

We have briefly discussed what we have labeled the politics of widow remarriage before discussing the politics of infant bestowal, although logically it might appear that infant bestowal should be taken up first. We have followed this order because, in Tiwi life, infant bestowal was reserved for fathers, and a Tiwi was at least a middle-aged man before he became a father at all. Before he could have a daughter to bestow, he had to be the father of one; and before he could become a father, he had to have a baby girl bestowed upon him and wait for her to grow up to child-bearing age. The much-married Ki-in-kumi did not have his first actual daughter (as distinct from wives' daughters begotten by previous husbands) until he was forty-five, and Enquirio was closer to fifty than to forty when his first real daughter was born. We are inclined to call such daughters free or unencumbered daughters since the step-daughters brought into a man's household by widows, even young widows, were already bestowed by act of the widows' previous husbands and the new husband's control over their marriage was therefore encumbered by the dispositions made by his predecessors.

Thus most men did not have and could not expect to have any free or unencumbered daughters to bestow until they were well into their forties. By that time a man was a prisoner of his past. When at last he had free daughters he was no longer a free man but a junior elder with a mass of obligations both to older men and to younger men, which he had contracted in the previous twenty or thirty years. Even his initiation, which had started when he was only about fifteen, left him under obligation to the older men who had initiated him. Any bestowals he had received had almost necessarily come to him from older men. In his thirties, it is true, he had operated in the widow remarriage area and put some older men under obligation to him by acting as their agent. But in his agency activities he had also contracted debts, usually in fee-splitting or log-rolling agreements with other agents of about his own age. Thus all his past activities, from his initiation at fifteen until the arrival of his first free daughter at (let us say) age forty-five, were on balance a story of obligations contracted and debts of gratitude assumed in his career of upward mobility. The more successful he had been up to now, the stronger the pressure on him to begin paying off those who had helped him, since it was assumed that his very success was a clear indication of how much obligation he must have to other men, especially older men and contemporaries.

If this line of reasoning had been the only relevant one, a Tiwi of age forty-five just presented with his first free daughter would have had problem enough deciding which of his many obligations to liquidate first by his bestowal decision for that daughter. Unfortunately he was at the age when he had to consider the future as well as the past. Some of his old obligations were to men who were very old and unlikely to live much longer. Others were to men of his own age with whom he had been partners ten years before, but by now it was clear that some of these would never amount to much and paying them off would reap no dividends for the future. Failure to meet the obligation might incur their enmity, but in view of their lack of success, perhaps their hostility was a lesser evil. In 1929, Gitjara, who had needed L. F. B. to get his own career launched, was ready to drop him as a partner now that Gitjara had attracted favorable notice in the form of two bestowals. The junior elders, though obligated to older men like Ki-in-kumi, were not bestowing their scanty free daughters on the older men but upon each other while waiting for the power alignment in Malau to change with Ki-in-kumi's death. Perhaps the clearest case of the pull between the obligations of the past and the planning for the future in the bestowal of free daughters was provided by Merapanui. He was a man who owed or thought he owed very little to his elders. None of them had ever bestowed a girl on him, and he reached fifty with nothing but an ancient widow. The fortunate death of an elder brother had suddenly provided him with bestowable daughters rather later in life than the average. By 1929 he had been able to bestow no less than four, and every one of them went to men much younger than himself and in other bands. Merapanui, being relatively free of old debts, was investing his daughters in young men with a future, but unlike Ki-in-kumi who had invested most of his daughters in one younger man, Padimo, old Merapanui believed in diversifying his investments.

Thus the politics of bestowal marriage were just as complicated as the politics of widow remarriage but, since a man was ten or more years older when he became involved in the former than when he became involved in the latter, a rather different set of motivations prevailed. At thirty-five as a mobile operator in the widow field, a man was trying to launch a career, and if he had no obvious assets—no living sisters or mother or important mother's brothers—he was often trying to launch it on a shoestring. By forty-five the same man was well along in his career and was a junior elder—the head of a household with at least one young wife in residence and a man beginning to have bestowable daughters of his very own. He now saw tribal politics and reputation building in different perspective from the way they had looked to him ten years earlier. Then he had put his services and his wits and his diplomatic skills at the disposal of older men in order to gain favorable notice from the elders. But now that he was an elder himself, albeit still low in the pecking order of elders, he was no longer their satellite but rather one of them and therefore in competition with them. Now he no longer wanted to build up his client's business; he wanted to build up his own household and his own influence. With the arrival of his first free daughters he was no longer content to work for and accept the leadership of older clients; he was in business as an elder for himself. His free daughters were therefore bestowed not as acknowledgments of his obligations to older men but as inducements to younger men to accept him as their patron. With his first free daughters a man was in position to become emancipated from the dominance of the elders because with the arrival of those daughters he could start bidding against them for the allegiance of men younger than himself.

One of the neatest examples of the switch in life career was provided in 1928 by the case of Tomitari. All Tiwi life careers and marriage arrangements were so tangled that one was delighted to find a relatively open and shut case. Some of the principals involved were relatives of Padimo, who was originally a Rangwila before Ki-in-kumi, his patron, lured him to Malau. Padimo and three sisters were the children of a Rangwila man and woman whom for simplicity's sake we will call Padimo's real father and real mother. The father bestowed the three girls on another Rangwila named Inglis who was about the same age as himself. (If we tried to answer *why* he did, the case would no longer be simple.) Padimo's father died while the four children were still young, and their mother remarried a relatively young man named Tomitari. This occurred in about 1914 and the situation then was as follows:

GENEALOGY I
THE INGLIS-TOMITARI RELATIONSHIP 1914
(Males are in italics; ages are in brackets)

| Padimo's Father (just dead) | 1. = | | Padimo's Mother (40) | = | 2. *Tomitari* (30) |
| *Inglis* = (44) | Sister I (21) | *Padimo* (20) | | Sister II (13) | Sister III (10) |

Fifteen years or so later, all parties were still alive; the two youngest sisters had joined Inglis as wives and all three sisters had borne children to him, including girls. Thus the situation in 1928-29 was:

GENEALOGY II
(1928-29)

Padimo's Mother (55)	=	*Tomitari* (45)
Padimo		Sister I wife of *Inglis* (59)
		Sister II wife of *Inglis*
		Sister III wife of *Inglis*
		↓
		Daughter A (11)
		Daughter B (8)
		Daughter C (5)
		Daughter D (2)
		Daughter E (1)

The three sisters of Padimo had borne five daughters to Inglis and as they were successively born Inglis had bestowed the first three on Tomitari. He did not bestow the fourth or fifth nor any of his daughters by other wives.

The master clue to the whole matter was the marriage in 1914 of Padimo's widowed mother to Tomitari, then little more than thirty. His function had been to act as trustee or stand-in for Inglis' interest, not in the widow but in her daughters who had been bestowed on Inglis by their dead father. The young Tomitari as step-father of the girls had to ensure their safe delivery to Inglis' household. (One was there already but the other two were not.) Tomitari accomplished his mission, acquiring the widow, of course, as a wife in the process; the girls arrived safely in Inglis' household and Inglis paid off handsomely by bestowing their daughters on his honest agent who had held off the competitors.

But by 1923 or thereabouts Inglis had stopped paying off. Tomitari by then had received three bestowals from Inglis. (Actually he had received about six, but three died in infancy). Moreover, he was no longer a young man but was entering the junior elder class and, having received wives from other sources than Inglis, was getting to the point where he would soon have free daughters of his own. He had no intention of performing any more services for Inglis who was now nearly sixty. Hence Inglis had not bestowed any daughters on Tomitari since 1923; those of his daughters who had been born since that year were bestowed on men other than Tomitari and men who were younger and less successful than he.

As we see it, the deals involving widows, particularly the pay-offs to young agents for acting to promote the interests of older men, had distorted what might be called the pure theory of Tiwi bestowal. According to the pure theory, mothers' brothers bestowed their daughters on selected sisters' sons, and the older man who gave a young man a wife and became his wife's father, was performing a kindness toward a favorite nephew for which the nephew should be grateful. But the Inglis-Tomitari operation shows how the theory had become distorted in practice. In order that Inglis might have some young daughters whom he would be free to bestow on his favored young nephew, Tomitari, in 1914 he had had to arrange the young man's marriage with an elderly widow to ensure safe delivery to him (Inglis) of some young wives who would bear him those daughters. Everything went smoothly and no slip-up occurred, yet by the time Inglis was in a position to give a wife to his favored young nephew, he found that the latter was no longer a dependent young man but a successful junior elder competing with him in his own field of identifying and using talent among the younger men. Tomitari's first daughter, born in 1927—not to any daughter of Inglis but to an older wife— was bestowed by its father on the distant but very promising Gitjara, a man of thirty-two. Gitjara was thus selected by Tomitari as a promising satellite at about the same age as Tomitari in 1914 had been selected by Inglis. Moreover, Tomitari by this time, far from being the grateful nephew of old Inglis (as the theory stipulated), was looking forward with anticipation to the old man's death, since when that occurred, among the widows of Inglis would be the three sisters of Padimo of whom he was still the nominal father. It was by acting as their step-father when they were children that he had got his own career started. They were indeed the foundation stone of his own career and, having profited so much from them as children, he was keenly interested in their redisposition whenever Inglis' death should put them on the market again. Thus he was simultaneously the husband of some of Inglis' daughters and nominal father of some of Inglis' wives. In the first status, he was expected by the theory to be a grateful son-in-law of Inglis; in the second status, the facts of Tiwi life required him to see Inglis' death as providing him with an opportunity to derive some new benefits for himself from his position as nominal father of the three wives of Inglis whose delivery to Inglis' household he had himself engineered.

Thus the politics of bestowal cannot be separated from the politics of widow remarriage. Every case of one had endless repercussions in the other. Sisters' sons who were promised young wives by their mothers' brothers were always too old to be grateful by the time the bestowal occurred or by the even later time when the bestowed child was old enough to come into residence.

Mothers' brothers, in turn, were unable to endow their nephews any earlier because they as younger men had been caught in the same trap. The only way out was by deals in which older men and younger men collaborated. Ideally such collaborative efforts should always have been between mothers' brothers and sisters' sons, but amid such fierce competition and endless log rolling this was not possible, and in many cases the mother's-brother—sister's-son relationship was a *result* of collaboration between older man and younger man rather than a cause. The bond arose from the deal rather than from their original kinship, particularly when the two men involved were very close in age.

The collaborative deals between older men and younger men were essentially designed to compensate for the older man's inability to bestow a young wife upon the younger man at a reasonable age. As was stated before, not until he was about forty-five would the older man have a free or unencumbered daughter. By then his younger collaborator and satellite had attracted the attention of older and wealthier men with many unencumbered daughters. After performing all his services to Inglis, young Tomitari had not had to depend on him for his first bestowal. A wealthier man than Inglis had reached over Inglis' head, so to speak, and bought Tomitari's allegiance by the bestowal of a young wife who provided Tomitari with a free daughter several years earlier than any child the daughters of Inglis could provide. With this first unencumbered daughter, Tomitari promptly bid for the allegiance of Gitjara. Put in terms of allegiances, Tomitari had from 1914 until about 1923 been the henchman of Inglis. During those years he passed from about age thirty to age forty, and his main patron was Inglis, who passed from about forty-four and on the fringes of the elder group to about fifty-four and accepted among the elder group. Then—and this was typical of the shift of allegiance that occurred in most life careers—a senior elder more wealthy in wives and daughters than Inglis bid for Tomitari's allegiance, and Tomitari became his henchman. Five years later, in 1928, Tomitari was a coming junior elder in Rangu and a man of influence in his own right. His oldest bestowed wife had already borne him a daughter whom he used to make Gitjara *his* henchman. The three wives (daughters A, B, and C) of Inglis were nearing the stage when they would join his household and he had other bestowals from other quarters. His relation to Inglis was no longer that of henchman but of rival, since they were now both successful elders in the same band and competitors in the struggle to make younger men dependent on them. Far from bestowing any more daughters on Tomitari, Inglis was bestowing his daughters (now plentiful) on men of Gitjara's generation (though not on Gitjara). Having more free daughters than Tomitari, he had more men of that generation to patronize, but since Inglis was sixty and Tomitari only forty-five, time was obviously on the side of the latter.

Thus the crux of the Tiwi system of influence-satelliteship-marriage arrangement-wealth centered around what happened to a man in his thirties. This is what we meant when we said earlier that old men with many daughters bestowed them on young men who looked to them like "comers." Old men with many free daughters were usually men well over fifty. "Comers" were men in their thirties. In so choosing the "comers," the old and wealthy men reached right over the junior elders and the forty-year-old group down to the ranks of the young operators. In this way we may say that the real power group, the successful old gerontocrats, chose their own successors. They chose young men twenty or more years younger than themselves (as Ki-in-kumi chose Padimo) because men at such an age were not rivals or competitors. A man so chosen in his thirties could be already powerful and fairly wealthy by his middle forties (like Tomitari in 1928) and very wealthy in his fifties. Such men went up fast because of their selection by the group in power. Those not so chosen had to go up the hard way by accumulating what position and influence they could by manipulations of the few available females not controlled by the wealthy old men. The "haves" left a small minority of women available to the "have-not" men to keep them quiet, but the great majority of females were concentrated in the hands of a few old men and these old men chose their own successors. Thus the Tiwi system actually deserves to be called a primitive oligarchy as much as it deserves to be called a gerontocracy. It was run by a few old men who ruled it not so much because they were old but because as young men they had been clever and then had lived long enough to reap the rewards of their cleverness. These rewards made up Tiwi wealth—many wives, much leisure, many daughters to bestow, many satellites and henchmen, and much power and influence over other people and tribal affairs.

4

The Collective Life

Legal Affairs

THE MOST SATISFACTORY overall view of Tiwi culture is that, within the general framework of mainland patterns, it had developed along its own distinctive lines. Some of these distinctive lines of development are traceable to the relatively favorable food and rainfall situation; others are traceable to the absence of neighbors. The unusually large polygamous households are, we think, attributable to the good food supply. But the large households of the Tiwi, economically efficient as we judge them to have been, involved certain social costs, the most obvious of which was the enforced celibacy of the younger men. This compulsory celibacy did not, of course, mean chastity. Not only were there the endless charges of seduction against young men, but there was also the more objective fact that most young wives continued to become pregnant with monotonous regularity, no matter how ancient and senile their husbands. (The Tiwi belief that babies came from spirits prevented pregnancies from being used against young wives as proofs of unfaithfulness.) Despite the numerous cases of seduction or alleged seduction, few young men ever took the most straightforward way of escaping from their state of compulsory celibacy—namely, abducting a young wife and running off with her. Here we encounter the other factor of the Tiwi natural environment that explains so much about their cultural development—and that is the absence of neighbors. Young men did not elope with young wives because there was no place to elope to. On the mainland such elopements were common, and the couple sought refuge with a neighboring tribe. But an eloping Tiwi couple could only take refuge with other more remote Tiwi bands where the system was the same as that which they had rebelled against back home, and the people with whom they sought shelter were interrelated with those whom they had defied back home. Hence, no matter where they fled, the Tiwi system, embodied in a war party of the girl's husband's friends and relatives, soon caught up with them. Several cases of such elopements occurred during the period of fieldwork, including the case of one young couple (Peanut and Jumbo's wife) who made repeated attempts to elope over a period of several years. But despite the relaxation of standards that white contact had brought, as long as they remained on the islands these violators of the system were soon forced back into conformity by outraged public opinion and its punitive sanctions. Unless he fled to the mainland with his girl, the young bachelor who stole an old man's young wife had to restore her sooner or later to her rightful husband. Under pre-white conditions they could not flee to the mainland; if they tried, they both probably drowned on the way or at least were never heard of again.

Thus the isolation of the Tiwi made the rule of the gerontocracy much more absolute, and the enforcement of it much more effective than was possible for any of the mainland tribes where violators of the rules could skip across the border. Tiwi bachelors had to be satisfied, by and large, with casual and temporary liaisons and even in these, because of the constant suspicion of the old husbands and the constant spying and scandalmongering of the old wives, they had to be prepared to be often caught and, when caught, to be punished. Thus we come to another of the main emphases in Tiwi culture—the enormous frequency of disputes, fights, duels, and war parties arising directly or indirectly out of cases of seduction. If we may call this area of life the legal area, then over 90 percent of legal affairs were matters in which women were in some way involved.

THE DUEL   The Tiwi formula for handling seduction was very straightforward and clear-cut in its formal outline. Since senior men had young wives and young men had not, seduction was necessarily viewed as an offense by a young man against a senior man. Hence the charge was always laid by the senior and the younger man was always the defendant.[1] At night in camp the accuser hurled his charges at the offender. We described earlier the alternatives available at this stage to both parties. Two of those alternatives were for the old man to press the matter to a public "trial," either the next day, if the camp was already a large one, or else on the next occasion when both men were present in a big gathering.

The basic shape of all Tiwi trials was standardized in the form that we have been calling the duel. Everybody present—men, women, children, and dogs—formed a rough circle in an open space, sitting or standing according to their degree of excitement at the moment. At one end stood the accuser, the old man, covered from head to foot in white paint, with his ceremonial spears in one hand and a bundle of the more useful hunting spears in the

---

[1] Under pre-white conditions this had to be so. After the arrival of the Catholic missionaries, some young men through Mission manipulation got a young wife at an age that would have been impossible earlier. This resulted in an occasional case around the Mission where a *young* husband charged a man older than himself with seducing his wife. The resulting duel, with an older man as defendant, was regarded by the Tiwi as both embarrassing and ludicrous, perhaps analogous to the average American's attitude toward female professional wrestlers. (See Hart 1954 for a case of this sort, the duel of Bob v. Louis.)

other. At the opposite end stood the defendant, with little or no paint on him, perhaps holding a hunting spear or two in his hand (a sign of insolence), perhaps holding only throwing sticks (less defiant, since the stick was an inferior weapon more appropriate to young men), or perhaps entirely weapon-less (a sign of proper humility and the deference to his seniors that all bachelors ought to show in such situations). The accuser, with many gestures, particularly with much stamping of the feet and chewing of the beard, told the young man in detail precisely what he and all right-minded members of the community thought of him. This angry, loud harangue went into minute detail, not only about the actual offense, but the whole life career of the defendant, and paid particular attention to occasions in the past when the old man even remotely, or some of his relatives, even more remotely, had performed kindnesses toward either the young man or some of his relatives. It is difficult to summarize briefly one of these harangues, but the general formula, subject to much variation by each individual accuser, appeared to be the building up of as much contrast as possible between the criminal or antisocial character of the young man's actions and the fact that he was a member of a network of interpersonal relationships in which mutual aid and reciprocal obligations were essential. The Tiwi orators, of course, did not put the matter in such abstract terms. They listed the long catalogue of people who had done things for the young man since his birth, and for his ancestors and relatives, until the catalogue took in practically the whole tribe—past, present, and future. And what had he done to repay his obligations to all these people? "Why, the miserable, ungrateful wretch spends his time hanging around my camp, etc., etc. And not only my camp, but last year it was widely believed that he was indulging in similar actions around the camp of my esteemed fellow-elder, So and So." We do not think that we are overintellectualizing the content of these harangues if we say that they involved the old man's reminding the young man of his debt to society, and his attempting to convey the idea that social life needed mutual aid and trust between all its members.

After twenty minutes or so of this sociological abuse and blame pinning, the old man threw aside his ceremonial spears and began to throw his hunting spears at the defendant. This active phase of the duel conformed to a stereotyped pattern which in some respects resembled baseball. The old man stood about ten feet farther away from the young man than the pitcher stands from the plate. The young man had to avoid being hit by the spears. To do this he was permitted to jump from side to side or into the air, or to duck, but he was expected always to land on approximately the same spot as he had been standing on when the first spear was thrown. Thus there was no marked strike zone, but an implied one. If the accused jumped well away from the strike zone, he was jeered by the crowd. If the old man was wild, he was jeered too, but more respectfully. Under such rules a modern baseball hitter, having no bat in his hand to worry about, would almost never be hit by a pitched ball, and the Tiwi young men were similarly never likely to be hit by an old man's spears. The main danger was the spear that pitched in the dirt. Although clearly outside the strike zone and hence an indication that the old man was really wild, such a spear was apt to carom off the ground at an unexpected angle and inflict a severe wound before the spectators (as collective umpires) had time to call it—in which case the duel was over and the accused was punished.[2]

Apart from those that unpredictably deflected off the ground, or even off a neighboring tree, the young man could dodge the old man's spears indefinitely if he wanted to. He was much younger and hence almost invariably in much better shape than the older man. But if he did this, the old man soon began to look a little ridiculous, and Tiwi society thoroughly disapproved of young men who made old men look ridiculous in public. Continued dodging and jumping and weaving of the body, no matter how gracefully they were done, were not prolonged by any young man who hoped in time to become a respected elder himself. The elders in the last analysis controlled bestowals, and holding one of them up to public ridicule was sure to antagonize all of them. So the young man, having for five or ten minutes demonstrated his physical ability to avoid being hit, then showed a proper moral attitude by allowing himself to be hit. This took even greater skill in bodily movement. Trying to lose a fight without making it too obvious to the crowd and without getting hurt too much oneself is a problem that confronts some professional athletes in our own culture, and few of them do it with as much skill as the younger Tiwi in the same situation. A fairly deep cut on the arm or thigh that bled a lot but healed quickly was the most desirable wound to help the old man inflict, and when the blood gushed from such a wound the crowd yelled approval and the duel was over. The young man had behaved admirably, the old man had vindicated his honor, the sanctity of marriage and the Tiwi constitution had been upheld, and everybody went home satisfied and full of moral rectitude. Seduction did not pay.

This was the Tiwi duel as it ideally should be conducted, and in perhaps as many as two-thirds of all such disputes it was so conducted. Divergences from this form clearly arose from the unpredictability of human beings and their fondness for trying to exercise choice instead of following a set pattern. Though the dice were heavily loaded against them, some Tiwi young men chose defiance instead of repentance. There were various avenues of defiance open to them. The mildest was to refuse to allow the old man's spears to hit the target. Slightly more brazen were the young men who turned up at the beginning of the duel with throwing sticks or hunting spears in their hands, even though they used these not to throw but to knock aside contemptuously the spears of the old man. More brazen still was the young man, rare but not unknown, who went so far as to throw missiles back at the older accuser. All such attempts to defy the traditional pattern of the duel met with the same response, and that very quickly. The duel began as usual with the two antagonists facing one another inside the circle of spectators. As soon as it became apparent that the young man was not conforming to the normal pattern of meekness and nonretaliation, there would be immediate activity on the

---

[2] Two cases of broken legs below the knee within six weeks of each other in 1928 give some indication of the force with which such badly aimed spears would bounce off the ground.

sidelines. Two or three or four senior men would leave the spectators and range themselves alongside the accuser, spears in hand. Other senior men would quietly leave their seats and sit down in the audience alongside close relatives of the young defendant, particularly his full brothers or his father, if they were present, and gently lay restraining hands upon them. Within a few minutes there was no longer an old man facing a young man but as many as four or five old men facing one young man, and no sign of support for him. His close male relatives would keep their seats or (more often) allow themselves to be led away as if they did not want to witness what was coming next. Never, in any of these cases, did any supporter of the young man step into the ring and line up with him. He remained an isolate, faced by several older men, and of course he had no chance. It was easy to dodge the spears of one opponent, since they had to be thrown one at a time; it was impossible to dodge the spears of more than one, since they could be thrown more or less simultaneously.

Usually this baring of its teeth by society-at-large was enough. The group of elders did not need to throw many spears simultaneously. The accused capitulated by throwing aside his spears or throwing sticks, or if the defiance had been only of the mildest form—namely, an undue prolongation of the dodging—he allowed his accuser to score a direct hit and the duel ended in the normal way. In the rare cases of the accused refusing to give up, even when confronted by a menacing line of several elders, a concerted volley or two from them quickly knocked him out, and in pre-white days, usually killed him.[3] Crime thus paid even less for the accused who chose defiance than it did for the accused who allowed himself to be wounded in a duel by a doddering ancient three times his age. The greater the amount of defiance, the more clear it became that the doddering ancient, acting ostensibly as an outraged husband, was the responsible agent of society dispensing public justice. If he needed help, all responsible elders went to his aid, and the kinsmen of the accused stood aside and let justice take its course.

WARFARE   Apart from the occasional castaways and the very occasional other visitors such as "Malays," the Tiwi in pre-white times had nobody to fight with except each other. Duels of the type we have just described were their only formula for settling disputes, and these occasionally became sufficiently broadened to warrant being called warfare. The expedition of Tiklauila and Rangwila to the country of the Mandiimbula which was listed in Chapter 2 among the travels of Tu'untalumi in 1928 was an example of this sort of activity. At least half a dozen senior members of the two first-named bands had disputes with various individuals among the Mandiimbula. Some of these were seduction cases but some of them involved charges by elder against elder,

---

[3] Since the coming of white administration, the Tiwi have found that when a man is killed in a native duel, there is a strong likelihood that white policemen will appear and will drag some of them off to Darwin where incomprehensible proceedings called murder trials then take place. To avoid such nonsense, since about 1925 they have tended to use throwing sticks rather than spears in their fighting. Throwing sticks, while dangerous, seldom kill people outright and as long as nobody is killed, the police in Darwin show no interest in native fights on the islands.

of nondelivery of bestowed daughters, or other types of broken promises. Some of these cases had been going on for years, and settlement of them at the level of the individual duel had failed. The aggrieved individuals in the two Bathurst Island bands therefore pooled their grievances, persuaded many of their relatives and friends who were not aggrieved to join them, and a large party of men of all ages set off for the Mandiimbula territory.

This party, comprising about thirty fighting men all heavily armed and all wearing the white paint indicative of anger and hostile intent, was a "war" party, and its coming to their territory was recognized as such by the Mandiimbula. On arrival at the place where the latter, duly warned of its approach, had gathered, the war party announced its presence. Both sides then exchanged a few insults and agreed to meet formally the next day in an open space where there was plenty of room. After a night mostly spent by both sides in individual visiting and renewing old acquaintances, the two armies met next morning in battle array, with the thirty Tiklauila-Rangwila warriors drawn up at one end of the clearing, and about sixty local warriors at the other end. Immediately the familiar patterns of the duel imposed themselves. A senior individual on one side began a harangue directed at an individual on the other. When he ran out of breath, another individual began his complaint. Since each accused Mandiimbula replied individually to the charges made against him, the whole proceeding remained at the level of mutual charges and replies between pairs of individuals. Angry old men on both sides often seemed to be trying to find a basis that would justify or provoke a general attack by one group upon the other, but always failed to find it because of the particularity of the charges. The rules of Tiwi procedure compelled the accuser to specify the sources of his charges and his anger, and these always turned out to be directed not at the Mandiimbula band, but at one, or at most two or three, individual members of that band. And when another old man took the center of attention, his anger would be directed at quite different individuals. Hence when spears began to be thrown, they were thrown by individuals at individuals for reasons based on individual disputes. Unlike the seduction duels, however, these duels occurred mostly between two senior men, and the danger of a direct hit was much reduced because of the poor marksmanship of both parties. On the other hand, the danger of somebody getting hurt was increased because a fight between two old men was likely to spread as other old men were drawn into it to support one or the other side—in which case, a wild melee occurred with badly thrown spears flying in all directions. This was probably a good thing, because soon somebody was bound to be hit, thus ending the fight. Not infrequently the person hit was some innocent noncombatant or one of the screaming old women who weaved through the fighting men, yelling obscenities at everybody, and whose reflexes for dodging spears were not as fast as those of the men.

As soon as somebody was wounded, even a seemingly irrelevant crone, fighting stopped immediately until the implications of this new incident could be assessed by both sides. For the crone was never really irrelevant; she was somebody's mother and somebody else's wife and somebody else's sister and therefore the question of who threw the spear that wounded her gave rise to a new series of wrangles which had to be integrated into all the old ones. A man who had been quietly sitting, minding his own business and having no quarrels with anybody, would suddenly leap into the center of the stage and announce that the damaged old lady was his mother and therefore he wanted the hide of the rat that had damaged her, and a whole new argument was in progress.

If the person wounded in the first flurry of spear throwing was a senior male, that similarly led the arguments off in some new direction since his kinsmen in *both* war parties felt compelled to support him or revenge his wound or inflict a wound on his wounder. Frequently it appeared that the original matters of dispute, which had brought the two war parties together in the first place, were forgotten and lost in the new disputes and fights that originated on the field of battle. Such a view was supported by the frequency with which one found at the end of the day that the main casualties and the main headline performers had been people who had gone to the field of battle in the morning with no quarrel with anybody, and not even wearing white paint. Even the most peaceful spectator in the most remote corner of the gallery was likely to find himself in the center of the ring before the day was over at a Tiwi "battle."

Despite this apparent confusion and near anarchy of procedure, however, the main outlines were quite clear. The bands were not firm political entities and therefore could not do battle, as bands, with each other. Everybody, on both sides, was interrelated in the same kinship system. An angry old Tiklauila, abusing and throwing spears at an angry old Mandiimbula, might have as the basis of his complaint the fact that the Mandiimbula father had promised but not delivered one of his daughters. Since Tiwi bestowals were from mother's brother to sister's son, the spear throwing was patently a case of a sister's son abusing his mother's brother, and the fact that the two men belonged to different bands was not germane to their dispute. The angry Tiklauila elder could not demand support from other Tiklauila *as Tiklauila* in the case at issue for it involved a dispute between kinsmen whose band affiliations were irrelevant to the subject matter. Mainly for this reason the so-called war party of one band against another band turned out to be only a loose collection of individuals, each with his own case to argue, who found it convenient, and safer, to travel together into the territory of another band and argue all their individual cases on the same day at the same place. Tiwi interpersonal relations were primarily kin relations between members of all bands; territorial loyalties were shifting ones, temporary and necessarily quite subordinate to kin loyalties. Hence warfare, in the sense of pitched battles between groups aligned through territorial loyalties, did not occur and could not occur among the Tiwi.

The confusion of the so-called battle itself was also due to the primacy of kinship and friendship ties. When a man with a grievance started his harangue on a battlefield, he was never quite sure of what support he would get or where it would come from. He was pretty much on his own, even though he had arrived there as a member of a large war party. This situation stemmed from the coexistence, on the one hand, of the intricate web of kinship that united everybody present and made the problem of who would support whom unpredictable enough, and, on the other, the intricate network of deals and promises and personal alliances and obligations that every senior Tiwi man had woven inside the kinship system. A Tiwi elder did not, for example, have one category of relatives called his mother's brothers; he had at least three different categories of mother's brothers. There were those mother's brothers who had given him nothing, those who had given him wives, and those who had promised him a wife but were dragging their feet on delivery, or even trying to renege on their promise. In pressing a case against one of this third category, an elder might quite conceivably alienate some of his mother's brothers of the second category. Nor could he be sure of the support of even his own brothers, since they were certainly cultivating, and possibly under-cutting him with, the same donors of daughters as he was involved with. Perhaps the nondelivery, which was the whole basis of his case against the mother's brother, had been instigated by his own brother trying to engineer a rebestowal of the girl to him. Because of the two networks, that of formal kinship obligations and that of marriage deals, two Tiwi seniors engaged in a dispute had no impartial body to whom they could submit their arguments about breach of contract. Disputes between a young man and an elder could be submitted to the publicly witnessed duel, since these were not breaches of contract but cases of trespass by the young men, and as such were crimes. Impartial public opinion upheld the old men and punished the young men every time. The old men's arguments with each other, however, could not be so adjusted, since they involved marriage deals (as distinct from seduction) and in marriage deals everybody was involved and nobody was impartial. Where any senior stood on any marriage deal in dispute depended on how that deal fitted into his own conniving. In that area of life, every adult man had his own axes to grind and a disinterested group of umpires was impossible to find.

Thus Tiwi battles had to be the confused, disorderly, inconclusive things they always were. They usually lasted all day, during which about two-thirds of the elapsed time was consumed in violent talk and mutual abuse between constantly changing central characters and satellites. The remaining third of the time was divided between duels involving a pair of men who threw spears at each other until one was wounded, and brief flurries of more general weapon throwing involving perhaps a dozen men at a time, which ended whenever somebody, even a spectator, was hit. As a result of this full day of violence, perhaps a few of the cases would be settled that night—by a father handing over his delayed daughter, or a man with a disputed wife relinquishing her to her rightful husband—but when the war party left next day to return home, the number of cases settled was likely to be less than the number of new feuds, grievances, and injuries that had originated during the day of battle. For not only did the participants carry away from the battlefield a vivid memory of all the physical wounds, intended or accidental, inflicted by whom on whom, but they also brooded long and suspiciously upon who had supported whom and why, either verbally or with spear in hand. In addition, all the incidents of the battle, in minute detail, were relayed to the rest of the tribe who had not been present, and many of these absentees would discover, among the proceedings, things they did not like or suspicious-looking actions on the part of some of their competitors or putative friends. These they would weave into their own strategies and store up for future use. An elder frequently found some basis for a new grievance against somebody in the events of a battle at which he had not even been present.

Finally, through all these disputes and hostile actions between senior men ran their united suspicion of bachelors. The only "battle" in two years between large groups drawn from distinct bands that had a clear-cut and definite final act was one fought in Rangu in late 1928. On that occasion, after disputing and fighting among themselves from early morning until mid-afternoon, all the old men present from both war parties gradually channeled all their anger toward one unfortunate young Mandiimbula bachelor whom they finally accused of going around from band to band creating misunderstandings between various elders. Several elders on both sides testified publicly that their mistrust of each other had started shortly after the bachelor in question had begun hanging around their households; whereupon the senior warriors of the two opposing armies had no difficulty in deciding that most of their suspicions of each other "were all his fault," and with great unanimity ganged up on the bachelor and quickly clubbed him into unconsciousness for being a troublemaker and a suspicion spreader. In the midst of battle the gerontocracy had reasserted its solidarity by finding a bachelor scapegoat upon whom to unload all their mutual suspicions and aggressions.

Religious Activities

If by religious activities we mean those beliefs and practices which pertain to unseen or supernatural forces, including rituals whose performance somehow affects those forces, then Tiwi religion readily crystallized around three focal points. These were: 1) their elaborate system of day-to-day taboos; 2) the elaborate set of beliefs and rituals pertaining to death; and 3) their complicated initiation ceremonies for young men. Add to these their myths and folklore about creation and their tribal past, and the whole of Tiwi religion has been covered. Space permits only brief mention of these three focal points.

TABOO   In earlier chapters we have pointed out several aspects of life in which Tiwi culture diverged sharply from what anthropologists have come to regard as Australian mainland norms and we have suggested that these differences from the mainland are most reasonably to be attributed to either Tiwi isolation or favorable food supply, or some combination of both factors. In their religious life this same line of explanation continues to have validity. To those familiar with the cultures of Australian tribes, perhaps nothing is so startling as to be told that the Tiwi almost completely lacked what we must call "positive" magic. Such familiar mainland practices as bone pointing or "singing" a man to injury or death were completely unknown on the islands, and though references to people dying through supernatural agency were often made, it was very hard to find any positive techniques or known practitioners of such techniques. Briefly the Tiwi may be said to have believed that magical acts were possible but to have lacked any knowledge of how to perform them. If, as anthropology is wont to teach, magic is used in the simpler societies to handle and control the unpredictable or mysterious areas of life, then this absence of magic among the Tiwi needs an explanation. Our hypothesis is that the Tiwi did not use magic in human relations because they had never invented magic for use in other unpredictable areas of life— for example, to control the natural world. And they had never invented magic to control their natural world because their physical environment was on the whole a satisfactory and not a hostile universe.

If we run through the areas of life that many of the simpler peoples use magical means to control, we find that many of them were not problems for the Tiwi. The rainfall and water supply were more than adequate; the food supply was good, needing only people to come and gather it; wild animals (except snakes and crocodiles) were unknown; tropical diseases (except yaws) scarcely existed; cyclones, tornados, and earthquakes were very rare, and thunder and lightning were no more frightening there than in, say, Chicago. Death, of course, is mysterious and unpredictable everywhere, but to handle that they had most elaborate burial and mourning customs that were not magical but collective rituals. Perhaps the most favorable feature in the whole friendly Tiwi universe was the absence of any neighboring tribe. Their cultural isolation removed all fear or suspicion of what the foreigners next door might be up to, and one gets the impression from the literature, though it has not been systematically explored, that the hotbeds of magic making and sorcery were areas of the primitive world, like Melanesia or Central Australia, where people were acutely conscious of their neighbors and always expecting magic and sorcery to be directed by them across the village or tribal boundaries. The Tiwi, having no neighbors, had nobody to be suspicious of except each other, and their suspicions of each other were mostly rational suspicions, of men motivated like themselves and using the same political tricks against each other.

The strongest support for the hypothesis that the Tiwi found their environment a friendly and reassuring universe to live in comes from their wide elaboration and reliance upon the negative form of magic called taboo. As a tribe they were magic free but taboo ridden. Their generic word for anything sacred or forbidden or untouchable was *pukimani*, a word which in its most common form referred to a state of special being in which a person or thing temporarily was. Thus mourners were *pukimani* for the period of their mourning, youths undergoing initiation were *pukimani* during the cere-monies, a woman who had just given birth was *pukimani* for a week or two afterwards. Dead bodies were *pukimani* until buried; graveposts were *pukimani* once erected on the grave; the names of dead people immediately became *pukimani* on their deaths and could not be used, and the same was true of all the names bestowed by a dead man on the children of his household and all the other words in the language that sounded similar to the name of the dead man.[4] All ceremonials and rituals were *pukimani* as were the main performers and the armlets, neck ornaments, and other ceremonial objects. People in a *pukimani* state had to observe all sorts of avoidances of and abstentions from everyday actions, particularly with regard to food and sex. Close relatives of dead people could not touch food but had to be fed by nonmourners. That pillar of rigid orthodoxy, Tu'untalumi, was virtually never able to feed himself but was in a *pukimani* state almost the whole year round and needed one of his wives to feed him. (Another advantage of a large household.) Certain spots in the bush or on the banks of streams were *pukimani* places; the dimly seen outline of the Australian coast was *pukimani* as was the ocean near Cape Keith where the Tiwi ancestors had first created the Tiwi world; and finally, the violation of a *pukimani* restriction rendered the violator *pukimani*.

Pukimani as thus applied to people, places, things, names, words, restrictions, and avoidances, meant both sacred and taboo, and was clearly one of that widespread class of words and concepts that is almost standard among the simpler societies. The only noteworthy thing about its Tiwi form is that *pukimani* was a state which people did not actively seek to enter but which happened to people regardless of their wishes. Furthermore, when a man found himself in a state of *pukimani,* his behavior was automatically prescribed for him and for the duration of his *pukimani* condition he observed his avoidances and his abstentions just as automatically as he dropped them when his *pukimani* period expired. When he became *pukimani,* he punctiliously fulfilled the requirements because if he did not, he was likely to be unsuccessful in his enterprises. Big men simply did not dare to be casual about the requirements lest their reputations suffer and they lose face and influence. Less successful men were occasionally explained as probably being secret violators. "His wives and daughters all seem to die young; he must have broken some *pukimani* restrictions sometime" was a reason often given for somebody's failure to be as successful as he might have been. It was noticeable in such explanations of nonsuccess that the failure, or in our terms the bad luck, was attributed to the violation of the taboos, never to the active displeasure of the spirits. The spirits simply did not figure in the picture.

Apart from the big ceremonial occasions, a Tiwi did not have much concern with religion in his everyday life except through some aspect of the *pukimani* system. It was only through *pukimani* that the sacred world impinged upon him at all for most of the year. Since *pukimani* was a condition that could not be actively sought but "just happened" to a person every so often by such common events as the death of a relative, his wife giving birth, or his

---

[4] When a man named Tibuki died in 1928, a crisis occurred at the Mission where the natives were supposed to make their requests in pidgin English. How could they now ask for tobacco, since that word was now *pukimani?*

sister's son being initiated, the attitude of a Tiwi toward the whole *pukimani* state was essentially a passive attitude. *Pukimani* behavior was something one accepted and conformed to when required; it was in no way an active attempt to change nature, people, food, gods, spirits, or anything else in the universe. It is therefore not unreasonable to conclude that since their *pukimani* system offered them no handle by which to seek actively to alter the universe in which they lived, the Tiwi found that universe to their liking as it was. Unlike the tribes of central Australia who lavished a lot of thought upon magical methods of improving the food supply or the rainfall, the Tiwi believed and acted on the belief that as long as they observed their *pukimani* taboos, the food would continue to be as abundant and the rains as regular as they had always been. The central Australians, by seeking to coerce nature through magic, suggest that they found nature unsatisfactory; the Tiwi, by relying upon passive taboo-observance alone, suggest rather that their relationship to nature was an acceptable equilibrium that they wanted to preserve, not change. And if everybody observed his *pukimani* taboos when required, that equilibrium would remain undisturbed. Hence the antisocial man in Tiwi was not the maker of individual magic (he was unknown, anyway) but the nonobserver of taboo. By his nonobservance he threatened to upset the normally satisfactory equilibrium between man and nature. For a senior Tiwi male to be charged publicly with breaking *pukimani* rules was a disgrace and a blow to his prestige and his position in public opinion. His behavior was possibly a sin against the spirits but it was certainly a shame in the eyes of his fellows. *Pukimani* observance was thus a matter of respectability to a much greater degree than it was a matter of pleasing the spirits.

DEATH   As was mentioned above, death is the natural phenomenon around which the Tiwi had woven their most elaborate web of ritual. The most frequent and most important Tiwi ceremonies were the mourning ceremonies, and they came in three sizes—small, medium, and large—depending on the age, sex, and importance of the dead person. The mourning ceremonies which drew the crowds were not held until some time after the death and burial. All bodies of dead persons were buried within twenty-four hours of their death by digging a hole near the camp where the death had occurred and placing the body, wrapped in bark, in it. Near most well-used camping spots there was already a graveyard marked by old graveposts, and the latest corpse was buried there or near there. Seldom was the body carried any distance for burial. If a person died even less than a mile from an old burial ground, there was little inclination to carry the body that far. He would be buried, instead, within perhaps a hundred yards of where he died. This had certain awkward repercussions for social organization, since occasionally a person died while away from his home district and, being buried where he died, his ceremonies were held and his posts erected in a district in which his immediate family did not live. Young men often used this to validate a change of residence, giving as their reason for living in a band territory in which they had not grown up, the location there of their father's graveposts.

To avoid constant use of the awkward phrase "mourning ceremony," we refer to it as the funeral though it took place some considerable time after the burial of the body. How long a time elapsed between the burial and the funeral depended upon the importance of the dead person. The more important the deceased, the longer it took after his or her burial to prepare for the funeral, both ceremonially and practically. Babies frequently had no funeral ceremonies at all, especially if they died very young and unnamed. Children were given small funerals, held within a month or so after the death, and the people present were merely the members of the local households. Young adult men and all adult women had funerals of medium size, and old men had the biggest funerals of all. Big funerals were rarely held in the wet season because of the height of the grass and bush and the consequent difficulty of travel. The season after the end of the rains (April-May-June) was a favorite time for funerals since by then people were moving again and there was then an accumulated backlog of funerals to be held for people who had died late in the previous dry season or during the wet. The mourning ceremonies of two or more people were sometimes held together; this obviously required that they be buried close together, although they need not have died at the same time. Seeking as usual to increase his importance in the public eye, a man might hold the medium-sized funeral of one of his children at the same time and place as the big funeral of an important elder—provided their graves were close together—even though two or three months had separated the two deaths.

The actual burial of the body immediately after death was usually a small affair attended only by whatever people happened to be in the vicinity. But some Tiwi ancients were on their last legs for months before they finally expired, and it was typical of Tiwi psychology that people should maneuver to be present when a death occurred. Until the anthropologist understood that even death had its political aspects, he could not understand why the Tiwi were always so anxious to hang around the camp of an old man who was taking an awfully long time to die. Since so very little happened at the actual time of death, this desire to be on the spot seemed merely morbid curiosity.[5] But it was not. A death immediately divided the whole tribe into two groups: a small group of relatives who automatically became mourners and therefore in a state of strict taboo, and the rest who were not sufficiently close to the deceased to have to assume a state of *pukimani*. The mourners, being *pukimani*, could do scarcely anything except weep and wail and gash their heads with stone axes. They could not touch the body or wrap it in bark; nor could they dig the grave, nor put the body in, nor fill in the hole. They had to ask non-mourners to carry out these tasks and thus became obligated to those non-

---

[5] How else was one to interpret the reluctance of Hart's party to move on, after spending three weeks waiting for old Tamboo to die, and the old man still lingered on? "Let's wait another day; maybe he'll die tomorrow" was the invariable response to suggestions that we move. "And if he does die, what will happen?" "Nothing; we'll move on then." But this was early in the fieldwork period, before Hart realized the all-pervasive character of Tiwi opportunism.

mourners for their services. Death, in other words, incapacitated the relatives, so the nonrelatives swarmed in to "help" them—that is, take advantage of their incapacity. A man who could say, "I helped to dig your mother's grave" had a hold for the rest of his life over the man or men to whom he could say it. Such a hold was not as strong, of course, as that of a man who could say, "I helped you get your first bestowed wife," but the difference of obligation was only a difference of degree. The Tiwi were always "helping" each other, but the man who was "helped" therefore "owed" something to his helper. At deaths, mourners mourned and nonmourners did the work; therefore the mourners "owed" the nonmourners, and such debts were carried on the same mental ledgers as other debts, such as marriage debts.

When deaths occurred suddenly and unexpectedly, the mourners had to choose their helpers for the burial from the relatively few people present at the time, and were thus often forced to become obligated to men they did not much relish being under obligation to. At the funerals the same bookkeeping mentality prevailed, but since these were not held until months after the death and burial, the chief mourners had time to select their helpers with care and political finesse. Satellites were very useful in this connection, since a man could ask his satellites to perform the necessary ceremonial services and thus get a return from them for the debts of gratitude they already owed him. This was one reason why a skillful Tiwi politician did not by any means select only close kinsmen for satelliteship. A death which made him *pukimani* was likely to make his close kinsmen *pukimani* also, hence he needed some satellites who were not close kinsmen.

In the interval between the burial and the funeral, the chief mourner, on behalf of all the mourners but fairly independently if he were a big man, allocated all the jobs that had to be done in preparation for the funeral. Everybody who came had to be fed by the mourners, and the collection and hoarding of the necessary food devolved on the women of the mourning households. Thus the mourners provided the food, but everything else necessary had to be prepared by nonmourners. The chief item among the ceremonial necessities was the graveposts. The prohibition on mourners approaching the body and the grave extended to the posts, and therefore the cutting, carving, erecting on the grave, and painting of these central features of the funeral ceremonies had to be carried out by nonmourners, "asked to cut the posts" by the chief mourner. Here there was much room for influence maneuvers. A big man acting as chief mourner for a dead relative wanted the funeral to be as lavish as possible, to show his own importance. But the more important the nonmourners he selected to cut the posts for him, the more he owed them for their services. Such a request was in the nature of asking a favor, and to ask a favor was to put oneself in a subordinate position, in terms of influence. The Tiwi power orientation was so ingrained that, even when acting as chief mourner, an elder could not avoid making his requests and allocating the ceremonial tasks so as to gain ground if possible, or at least not lose any ground, in the influence and prestige race.

The mourning ceremonies, though prolonged for several days of constant dancing and singing, were rather dull and monotonous, considered as ceremonial. The gaily colored posts erected right on the grave served as a sort of central altar. Every senior male sang and danced in turn " his own dance" and the rest of the men standing in a large circle acted as a major chorus. A large gap was left in the circle of men and into this gap and out again danced the women in a disorderly clump, as a sort of minor chorus. Most of the day was taken up with endless repetitions of these individually owned and individually performed dances which had no relation whatever to death or the deceased, but which each "owner" used on every ceremonial occasion. In addition, there were a few ritual performances that were special to the fact of death, including the grand finale of every mourning ceremony, when everybody present, led by the mourners, collectively charged the posts and then roared past them into the surrounding bush. This was done to drive the spirits away from the grave finally and forever and thus end the mourners' state of *pukimani.*

We have no space for further details of ceremonial, but enough has been said to indicate that mourning ceremonies, the biggest collective occasions of the Tiwi dry season, were as much political affairs as they were religious occasions. The connecting link was the state of *pukimani* in which death put the relatives. Men in a state of *pukimani* were at a disadvantage in social and political life while that state lasted. They had to ask other people to do things for them. They had to "pay" for these favors. At the same time they could not afford to be niggardly in running their relative's funeral. If they were, they would never live it down. In such an atmosphere we have to conclude that the spiritual welfare of the deceased was relegated to a minor place and that for the mourners the real climax of the days of frenzied grief around the posts came when the spirits were driven away from the grave into the bush and thus their own *pukimani* state, which had been such a political handicap to them for many months, came to an end.

INITIATION   Space permits only the barest mention of initiation, which was, along with mourning, the chief vehicle of Tiwi ritual. For females there were no initiation ceremonies, but for males it was a long drawn-out and elaborate affair, marked by successive stages or grades which began with the status of *Marukumarni,* which a boy entered when he was about fourteen, and did not end finally until he was around twenty-four. Here again we meet the ideology of debt and obligation. The group of men, necessarily older than himself, who initiated a youth thereby put him under obligation to them for the rest of his life. They "did something for him" and years later would bring it up if his subsequent behavior seemed to be directed against their interests. The obligations contracted in initiation, like obligations contracted at burials or mourning ceremonies, were woven into the kinship and influence systems; indeed the relation of a youth to the men who initiated him was often the beginning of a satellite-patron relationship that lasted half his life.

The initiation of a boy had to be undertaken by a group of men who were already fully initiated themselves and who stood to him in the relation of male cross-cousins. Preferably such men were either married to or likely to marry the boy's sisters, an easily met requirement since girls were "married" so much earlier than their brothers. Very senior and successful men did not bother as a rule with initiation sponsorship because it took too much of their valuable time. Hence in practice, most boys at the *Marukumarni* age were taken in hand by a group of men around 40 years of age who were at least betrothed to, if not already married to, the boys' sisters. Such men justified or rationalized their actions by stating that, as the husbands of the boy's sisters, they wanted their little brother-in-law to be made into a man in proper form. In fact, they were usually given the job by the boy's father, who, having bestowed daughters upon them, regarded it as a legitimate request to make of them. It was the duty of male cross-cousins to initiate their wives' little brothers, but in true Tiwi style the father had to request them to do it, and they counted it in their tallies of what they owed him and what he owed them.

Though the father instigated and stage managed the whole affair, he and his household were always thunderstruck when the cross-cousins—armed to the teeth and painted like a war party—arrived at his camp one evening and proceeded to carry off forcibly the yelling 14-year-old.[6] He had to be dragged literally from the bosom of his family, with his mother screaming and trying to hide him and the father pretending to resist the invaders of his household. From then on, until the final stage (*Mikingula*) at age 24-26, the boy was completely under the authority of the men who carried him off. During these approximately ten to twelve years, he spent much of the time alone with them in the bush where the group lived a monastic existence, as a small band of isolates, speaking to no one (especially not to females) and obtaining their own food. During these phases the tutors guarded the boy as if he were literally a prisoner and taught him all the things—chiefly ritual matters—that grown men should know. At intervals the youth was allowed to go home, on week-end leaves so to speak, but when at home he had to observe all the silences, the modest demeanor, the taboos and the austerities of the isolated life. In monastic language, he was under a strict rule of obedience to his tutors.

Breaking in on the long years of austerity, spent either in seclusion in the bush or in *pukimani* at home, were periodic collective ceremonies when the youth was ritually advanced from one stage of initiation to the next.[7] These were public ceremonies, witnessed by large crowds, and the more important of such transition ceremonies took place in January and February when the *kolema* yams were ripe. At these ceremonies the youths were handled in batches or classes, all the boys of one grade being ritually advanced to the next grade, and the top grade or final class being formally graduated as fully initiated men. The crucial grade—when the pubic hairs were forcibly pulled out and he was at last allowed to talk back a little to his tutors—was usually reached by a youth somewhere between his eighteenth and twentieth years, but

---

[6] See Hart 1955 for some further details of the tearing away of the boy from the bosom of his family.

[7] A full list of initiation grade names and their duration in years is given in Hart 1931.

he still had six years to go after that, not finishing the final grade of *Mikin-gula* until somewhere past the age of 24 or 25.

In contrast with the mainland initiation ceremonies, we think the most interesting point about Tiwi initiation resides not in the formal ceremonies but in the removal from the food-production units, for long periods of the year, of all the young males between the ages of 14 and 25. It is true that they did not spend *all* their time in seclusion and that after the age of twenty they remained mostly in their household camps, where they contributed to the household food production. Nonetheless, it remains clear that only a very well-off tribe could afford to allow so much time off from food production to all its young hunters. Tiwi fathers, it would seem, in arranging for the initiation of their sons to begin just when they were becoming productive hunters, were willing to sacrifice that productivity for less tangible advantages. The youths, secluded and guarded in the bush while getting an education, were not only out of the work force but were also out of the predatory-bachelor force. A Tiwi elder made sacrifices to "send his sons to college" but he breathed easier to know that the sons of the other elders were all there too.

All males without exception had to go through the full initiation cycle, and from the time of their first forcible seizure at the age of 14-15 to their final graduation at 24-26, they were in a state of *pukimani* and their personal names were strictly taboo to everybody in the tribe. Each youth was referred to only by his grade name, *Marukumarni* for the first year, *Mikingula* for the last four years, and so on. And here we return finally to a point which was mentioned much earlier—namely, the complete unimportance in tribal eyes of all males below the age of twenty-five. Until they had completed the final stage of initiation, Tiwi males were still boys; they did not even have names. Occasionally, when collecting genealogies and coming upon a reference to a young man, the innocent anthropologist would ask, "Is he married?" In tones of the deepest contempt the informant would reply, "That kid, how could he be married? He's still *Mikingula*." Though *Mikingula* was the stage typically reached by a man at about 20-21 and lasted for the next four years, to the Tiwi it was still a stage in the life of a boy. Not until he had finished as *Mikingula* could he step out into the world and life of men. How he spent the years immediately after finishing initiation decided how soon some senior man would think sufficiently highly of him to aid him in acquiring his first ancient widow.

5

Friend and Foe
(1600-1928)

O N NEARLY ALL SIDES, the emptiness of a great sea surrounded the Tiwi; to the south, the only path which might have led to the outside was blocked by the hostility of their nearest mainland neighbors. The Tiwi retained this isolation until the very end of the last century, even though for several centuries outsiders had been seen by them; ships passed along the coast and occasionally strangers landed or were cast ashore. Changes in the life on the islands were few, however, until about 1900, when the Tiwi began their integration into the modern world.

Hostility toward Outsiders (1600-1900)

Although in June of 1636 the sailor Pieter Pieterszoon in command of the ships *Cleen Amsterdam* and *Wesel* sailed along the western twenty miles of the north coast of Melville Island and named the region Van Diemensland,[1] our first real knowledge of the natives of Bathurst and Melville islands was gained by the Dutch expedition to this region in 1705 under Maarten van Delft. Men from his three ships spent about two weeks in surveying the north coast of Melville Island, the northern two-thirds of Apsley Strait between Bathurst and Melville islands, and the entire west coast of Bathurst Island.[2] They met natives several times and even allowed them aboard their ships.

Following this meeting between islanders and Europeans was a period during which the natives became extremely hostile to outsiders. Tiwi distrust of foreigners probably stemmed from these decades when the Portuguese on Timor were raiding Melville Island for slaves. Although very little has been

---

[1] Heeres 1899.
[2] *Ibid.* See also Mander Jones 1948 for some further data concerning Dutch knowledge of Melville Island.

published concerning this era, such lack of information should not be taken as a refutation of such practices; the Portuguese archives remain today the only major block of libraries concerning a European colonial power important in the East Indies which has not been examined for material relevant to the history of Australia. From what little is known we may conclude that the Portuguese stopped capturing Tiwi as slaves about 1800.[3]

Even before the Portuguese made their last raids on Melville Island, another type of stranger, the "Malays" (or as we would call them today, the Indonesians), began to have encounters with the Tiwi. It was the search for the Chinese delicacy, the trepang or sea slug, which annually caused the Malays to sail past Melville Island eastward to Arnhem Land and the Gulf of Carpentaria. Neither the free-lance trepangers nor those sailing out of Macassar in the fleet of the Radaj of Boni wanted to stop at Melville Island, and they considered their misfortune to be great if their proas happened to be wrecked on its coast. They, like other Indonesians blown in to the homeland of the Tiwi, had little chance of surviving, for the Tiwi normally speared such poorly armed intruders and asked questions later.

The nineteenth century was an era of decreasing isolation for the Tiwi; during it, the outside world was knocking hard and often on their door. In 1802, a French expedition under Baudin mapped the southwestern tip of Bathurst Island, although its members apparently did not make a landing. In 1818, a British ship under P. P. King made a detailed coastal survey of Bathurst Island and all except the southeastern coast of Melville Island. Then on September 26, 1824, the British founded Fort Dundas on northwestern Melville Island, the first European settlement in the tropical part of Australia. The British and the Tiwi did not make friends. The imaginative commander of this outpost of empire, Major John Campbell, tried to capture a Tiwi and teach him sufficient English so that he could tell his tribesmen that the British would shoot them if they did not stop spearing the Englishmen and their buffalo imported from Timor. One Tiwi was captured but escaped within a fortnight under cover of darkness; meanwhile the British mourned for their doctor and storekeeper who had gotten in the way of well-aimed Tiwi spears. No native learned English. The British, disillusioned by their perpetual battle with the Tiwi and with tropical decay, abandoned Fort Dundas on March 31, 1829. Four and a half years of exposure to the British had affected the Tiwi little.

But the Tiwi were not to remain without external intruders. Shortly before 1844 a Dutch ship was wrecked on their coast. In 1858, an English vessel was lost on Melville Island. In 1869, the city now known as Darwin was founded and ships began to pass Bathurst or Melville islands almost daily. In the 1880's two ships, the *Afghan* and *Northern,* went aground off the

---

[3] The following statement from George Windsor Earl's *The Native Races of the Indian Archipelago: Papuans* (London: Hippolyte Bailliere, 1853, p. 210,) is probably the most significant passage concerning the Portuguese relations with Tiwi: ". . . According to . . . the older inhabitants of Timor, Melville Island was only less a source of slavery than New Guinea, in proportion to its smaller extent of surface, at the period in which the slave-trade was encouraged or connived at by the European authorities . . . ."

southern coast of Bathurst Island. In 1886, the Australian government tried to erect channel markers on the southern shore of Melville Island, whereupon the Tiwi immediately "salvaged" both cloth and iron from them. During June and July of the same year the ship *Jane Anderson* was stranded on the shoals of first Melville and then Bathurst Island. Also in 1886, two Malay proas were wrecked on the north coast of Melville Island. That year was a great one for looting.

Occasionally visitors came ashore on the islands. The Stokes' survey party landed in the late 1830's, but saw no natives. A government party crossed Melville Island in 1887; the Tiwi speared its leader. In 1895, a government tourist party went to look over the ruins of old Fort Dundas; they kept their eyes open and no one was injured. In 1897, Joe Cooper, a buffalo shooter, tried to make a living from the Melville Island buffalo; he was speared and retreated to Darwin.

Tiwi treatment of outsiders prior to 1900 had been to rob them, spear them, kill them. This is not, however, the picture painted by modern Tiwi when talking of their past. They claim that their ancestors greeted each new group of strangers with the cry: *"Pongki! Pongki!"* (meaning, "Peace! Peace!"). But then it should be noted that before 1900 many a Tiwi peacemaker carried a spear between his toes. Yet under these circumstances the Tiwi world view did alter. First there were those changes which came from an attempt to understand the new objects which were suddenly thrust into the Tiwi world: the trade knives and axes given by Dutch navigators, the matchlock guns used by the Malays and probably the Portuguese, the rice given to Tiwi by the surveyors under P. P. King, the Indonesian water buffalo introduced by the British at their short-lived settlement, the coconut palms the English left behind them, the cups and plates from shipwrecks in the 1880's, and the flour tossed overboard to lighten foundering vessels. The Tiwi cherished iron knives and axes, readily recognizing their greater efficiency. The Tiwi begged for them; they stole them; and, when a spar washed ashore bound round with iron bands, the natives burned away the wood and took the iron away to grind into axes. The matchlock gun, and even the later flintlock, could be coped with; when one saw the flash, one ducked flat, just in case the weapon worked, and then rushed in to impale the stranger with a spear. Rice was useless; it looked like the larvae of the termite, which was not good for anything anyway. Buffalo were to be killed; they kept wallowing in the best waterholes. Coconut palms were a great disappointment; they were bigger than the local cabbage palm, but when cut down, did not have the same succulent interior. Plates were too much bother to carry around, but cups were worth saving for a while. Flour could be used for white paint, but it was not as good as the best white pigment near at hand.

Other modifications took place in Tiwi life before 1900 as a result of action by outsiders. Probably the greatest of these alterations came as a result of slave raiding, or "black birding" as it is called in the South Seas. The Tiwi always kept their young women hidden from strangers, even if they were just visitors from other bands. The old men rarely left camp. Therefore, it was the young males who went, or were sent, to try to satisfy their curiosity and to get iron from the Portuguese—and it was these young males who would make the best slaves in Timor. The anthropologist is left to wonder to what extent the removal of a disproportionate number of young men from a group might alter the form of the society. Is it possible that such happenings might be a factor which contributed to the dominance of the old Tiwi men and their near monopoly of wives? Could it be that the politics involved in wife trading were an indirect result of the Portuguese slave raiding? The possibility at least exists, and perhaps research in Portuguese archives will give us some clearer idea of how many young Tiwi men were carried off to Timor during this period. Present-day Tiwi, of course, remember nothing about it.

The Beginning of Friendly Contact
(1900-1928)

Today the Tiwi have been incorporated into the modern world as a part of the Australian nation, yet they came to understand outsiders, including Australians, through persons with many national backgrounds. Individuals who have helped to shape Tiwi views of non-Tiwi have been Indonesians, Filipinos, mainland natives from the Cobourg Peninsula, Frenchmen, and Japanese, as well as Australians from the southern parts of Australia.

The Tiwi were first drawn out of their hostile insularity by curiosity and the desire for iron, the same factors which had attracted them toward the Portuguese a century earlier. Iron looted from shipwrecks, channel markers, and the camps of casual visitors to the islands was not sufficient; the Tiwi desired a permanent avenue by which they could obtain the metal. The oldest Tiwi in the early 1950's stated that during the 1890's the Tiwi began to feel that opportunity was passing them by as they noted ship after ship sail in and out of Darwin; the islanders therefore came to the conclusion that they wanted a permanent European settlement in their midst, like the earlier Fort Dundas, for only in this way could they be guaranteed an uninterrupted source of iron.

About 1895, events began moving toward the establishment of a long-term European center on the islands. The vanguard of the movement was not European, however. In 1885, mother-of-pearl shell of commercial value was found on the bottom of Darwin Harbor. A few years of intensive diving by "Malay," "Manila," and Japanese pearlers soon worked out the Darwin beds, making it necessary for the growing fleet of pearling luggers to go further afield. They stripped the coast north of Darwin, moved on to the south coast of Melville Island, and finally began working the great shoals at the south end of Apsley Strait. Cautiously at first, the pearlers went ashore for water and firewood. Young Tiwi men became curious and paddled out to visit the luggers hove to just off the southern beaches in the neap tides. Aboard the luggers Tiwi youth had occasional meals, smoked tobacco, and were given iron tools. The Mandiimbula of southern Melville Island in particular began to look forward to the periodic visits of the luggers, for they brought a new source of iron and trinkets.

Joe Cooper, the Australian buffalo hunter who had been chased out of the islands on his first attempt in 1897, returned again a few years later having first kidnaped two Tiwi women so that his mainland native helpers of the Yuwatja (Iwaidja) tribe near Cape Don could learn the language. When they had, he returned with a strong mainland detachment and well equipped with guns and horses. By 1900, European firearms were efficient weapons and a Tiwi spearman no longer could expect to kill a man armed with a modern rifle. Cooper is said never to have gone unarmed in his fifteen or so years (from about 1900-1916) as "King of Melville Island."[4]

In retrospect it is apparent that the agent through whom the Tiwi learned of the outside world was not Cooper, the white man, but his companions the Yuwatja (Iwaidja). They were more numerous and more approachable than Cooper, and several of them even had Tiwi wives whom they had captured. Tiwi accounts of these captives are noteworthy. It was the young Tiwi men hanging around Cooper's camp who suggested to the Yuwatja that they go and capture, by force of arms, Tiwi females who had recently become widows. The young men were thus performing their customary role of agents in widow remarriage—but in this case for foreign clients.

Cooper and his Yuwatja camped at various localities on Melville Island until about 1916 when their last base, at Paru opposite the site of the Mission, was abandoned and he and his mainlanders withdrew from the islands. It was this last camp at Paru that was made headquarters by Sir Baldwin Spencer, the well-known Australian anthropologist, when he visited the Tiwi in 1912.[5]

While Cooper was at Paru he was also visited by a young Alsatian priest, Father Francis Xavier Gsell, M. S. C., who was contemplating establishing a mission on adjacent Bathurst Island. Cooper tried to discourage Father Gsell by telling him that the Bathurst Islanders had guns and were dangerous; apparently Cooper did not want any missionaries around his rough-and-ready establishment. But Father Gsell did not scare easily; in June 1911 he returned and built his mission station on the southeast corner of Bathurst Island, where it still stands today. Cooper left Paru permanently about five years later.

By 1916, five years after its founding, the Mission had two French priests, several French nuns and some Filipino workmen, and a lugger which ran to and from Port Darwin once a month. It was not until the nuns came that the local Tiwi put any trust in the missionaries; they could not understand why a man who claimed to be as important as Father Gsell claimed to be did not have any wives. When the nuns arrived, the Tiwi were more ready to accept the priest as "a big man" and began to bring their women around.

---

[4] Hardly a year goes by without a newspaper in Australia running a Sunday supplement article on Cooper's stay at Melville Island. Such stories often are titled "The King of Melville Island" and are normally extremely romanticized.

[5] Spencer 1914. Spencer's account of the Tiwi is remarkably inaccurate and confused. On this trip to the Northern Territory in 1912 he was without his usual collaborator, Gillen.

Thus Cooper with his well-armed retinue of mainlanders had made the islands safe for white men and introduced a desire for white men's goods, particularly tobacco. His retirement from Melville Island left the newly established Mission on Bathurst Island as the only source of supply for these goods. After World War I, however, another influence began to grow in importance. Large numbers of Japanese pearling boats came and anchored off the coasts of southern and southeastern Melville Island, where they traded with the local bands—the Yeimpi and Mandiimbula. These bands got tobacco and European-type food (flour, rice, tea, sugar) from the Japanese in quantities which the Catholic missionaries could not afford to provide; all the Japanese asked in return was access to young native women. Men who controlled many women—as fathers, as husbands, or as brothers—were thus in a favorable position to profit by the traffic with the Japanese.

Whereas the demands made by the Japanese on the Yeimpi and Mandiimbula for women were quite straightforward and uncomplicated, Father Gsell's demands on the bands of south Bathurst Island were somewhat more complex in their consequences. Many aspects of the old pattern of Tiwi life had to be abandoned to make them into Christians. To the missionaries, polygamy was sinful and could not be part of the new Tiwi life. Prenatal and infant bestowal had to be abolished. Marriages should be between agemates and should be arranged freely and solely by the couple involved. Such changes were the crux of Father Gsell's program, and the story of how he went about it has run in many a Sunday supplement in the cities of Australia under the title "The Bishop With 150 Wives."[6] Father Gsell did not try to convert or drastically change the behavior of the older Tiwi; he believed that they were too set in their ways. Rather, he built toward a distant day by working among the younger generation. When infant girls became widows, he purchased them from their fathers. Men with young widowed daughters and those with spare young wives sold such girls for axes, flour, tobacco, cloth, and trinkets. Such "Blackies," as they became affectionately called,[7] lived in the convent with the French (and later Australian) sisters. When such a girl reached the age of about 18, she was asked to choose one of the young single men for her husband. For his part in this excellent deal which provided him with a wife long before he would get one under the old tribal system, the young man had only to promise that he would never take another wife. Such a wedding was not a Mass, for neither party was Catholic. However, the children born of this new union were baptized and reared as Catholics. Later, a few of the girls who had been sold to Father Gsell before they were ten went through confirmation as did their youthful fiances. The first nuptial Mass between two such Tiwi took place in 1928.

---

[6] Father Gsell became Bishop of Darwin in 1938. He lived on in retirement to 1958, having seen in his lifetime the fulfilment of his dream of the Tiwi as a Catholic tribe.

[7] The Tiwi today strongly resent being called "African," "Negro," or "nigger," but they do not seem to mind being called "Blacks." The term "Blackie" for a young female is in general use by Mission school girls for themselves; it is in no sense derogatory.

When between the mid-1920's and the early 1940's the Japanese began to give trade goods to men for sexual access to their wives, Father Gsell's missionization program ran into competition. The Japanese gave the old Tiwi males a much better deal than did Father Gsell. The Japanese with their continuous payment for access to women poured into the households of these old men the same sort of goods which Gsell provided. But in the case of the Japanese, the goods were paid time and again over a matter of years and the old father or husband was kept permanently in tobacco and food. Thus, oddly indeed, the two chief outside influences which came to bear upon the traditional Tiwi system of marriage, after about 1920, were both agencies which were anxious (for entirely different reasons and ends) to "buy" young girls and pay their ancient husbands or fathers for relinquishing them; temporarily in the case of the Japanese, permanently in the case of the missionaries. The Tiwi could scarcely be expected to cease putting a high value on women, and upon control over women, under these conditions.

6

The Tiwi Today

Changes since 1930

THERE WERE in 1929 only two year-round settlements of outsiders which were significant to the Tiwi. One was Bathurst Island Mission, by then nearly twenty years old, the only permanent white-man establishment on the islands. It acted as the main exit point for travel to Darwin, the other focus of Tiwi life. There was also the large camp of Mandiimbula and Yeimpi on the south coast of Melville Island, which owed its existence to the sexual arrangement between the Tiwi and Japanese pearlers.

In the 1930's, the centers of Tiwi activity shifted somewhat. The Australian government successfully broke up the camp located on the south coast by transporting nearly all of the Yeimpi to Darwin and by sending patrol boats out to discourage the Japanese from frequenting the area. In about 1935, the Japanese moved their base for contact with the Tiwi north to the region of Garden Point, at the northern end of Apsley Strait, just beyond the ruins of old Fort Dundas. Around the great fresh-water pool on the beach at that locality there developed a Tiwi camp like that which formerly had existed on the south coast; however, the native bands involved were no longer the Yeimpi and Mandiimbula but the Malauila, Munupula, Wilrangwila, and Turupula of northern Bathurst and Melville islands. The government again attempted to control sexual activities between Tiwi and Japanese, but to get to this spot a patrol boat from Darwin had to travel along forty miles of indented coastline which amplified and seemed to project every throb of an engine toward the ears of the Japanese miles away. The patrol boats found that they could not sneak up on the pearlers unannounced and, therefore, could not catch them in the act of cohabiting with native women.

By the late 1930's, pressure from missionary and other humanitarian circles in the southern part of Australia forced the government to attempt to terminate, or at least to control, the trade pattern which had become established between the northern Tiwi and the Japanese. A government ration depot was founded at Garden Point about 1939 and many of the local Tiwi females were taken by the government to Darwin in order to stop their use by Japanese pearlers. However, by that time many Japanese half-castes had been born to the women.

In 1940, a new Catholic mission was established at Garden Point to care for these half-castes. This Melville Island Mission brought together not only the island part-aborigines, but also other Catholic half-castes from all over the Northern Territory. By late 1940, it became clear that the existence of a government depot for aborigines at Garden Point was incompatible with a policy aimed toward educating the adjacent half-caste children for life as members of the white Australian community. The government ration center was removed to Snake Bay. Also, by 1940, the government had begun to remove lepers from both Bathurst and Melville islands to a leprosarium on Channel Island in Darwin harbor. Here, over the following years, developed a community of Tiwi which often numbered as many as forty persons. At Channel Island they found themselves forcefully confined amongst natives from many mainland tribes. Tiwi who returned from Channel Island after years of residence there were more sophisticated in European ways than their fellow-tribesmen and found themselves agents of white Australian culture.

The winter (our summer) of 1941 was the last in which the Japanese came to Garden Point. The Catholic brothers who were there at the time viewed at least one extraordinary event in those months before Pearl Harbor. On this occasion, a man in the uniform of a Japanese naval officer was seen aboard the mother ship of the Japanese pearling fleet which called in at Garden Point; under Australian law neither ship nor officer were allowed within the three-mile limit. Pearl Harbor occurred a few months later.

The year 1942 brought modern warfare to the Tiwi. An American plane running out of the Philippines lacked enough fuel to get to Darwin; it landed on the small airstrip at Bathurst Island Mission. Then on February 19, 1942, Darwin was bombed. Japanese planes flew over Bathurst Island Mission on their way to commit what became "Australia's Pearl Harbor." Father McGrath, the local priest, recognized the raiders as Japanese and radioed his warning into Darwin twenty minutes before the horror commenced. The message went unheeded and the loss of life and property was great. Bathurst Island Mission was itself strafed, possibly for the attempt to warn Darwin. The bombing of Darwin left the Northern Territory in chaos. The white residents evacuated southward by any means at hand; in one case, two men drove a road grader seventy miles "down the track" before they felt safe enough to stop.

The disruption of the Tiwi community was as great as that of the white settlement at Darwin, although no Tiwi were killed in the bombing and strafing by the Japanese. The Catholic authorities realized that they could not guarantee a food supply to the natives, and the Tiwi families at the Mission were sent to the bush to support themselves. Tipperary, a Tiwi who was by 1942 an old hand in Darwin, told Pilling (1954) of the privation he had endured when he had taken to the bush and had not had a smoke for four months after the attack on Darwin. Many of the older Tiwi who were in Darwin during the bombing did not survive the war; the psychological strain and lack of sufficient food was too much for them. Genealogies show that an unusual number of deaths occurred among Tiwi between 1942 and 1946.

When Western food supplies again became available, the old Tiwi bush living seems to have departed. The Tiwi suddenly realized their full dependence upon the products which only the whites could provide. As the war came to an end and one after another of the temporary military bases were abandoned, the missionaries and the Tiwi salvaged what they could, transporting large amounts of corrugated iron to Bathurst Island Mission for native huts. The Tiwi were drawn together around the Mission in larger numbers than ever before, their camps ranging in a line along the Mission beach. The majority of the Tiwi, about 600, considered Bathurst Island Mission their home, although some of the young adult males spent most of the year in Darwin. About 50 islanders lived adjacent to the half-caste Melville Island Mission at Garden Point. Another 150 were permanently located at the government settlement at Snake Bay. The remaining Tiwi, about 150, were year-round residents of Darwin; over one hundred lived at Bagot Native Compound and at an unsupervised native camp at Point Gunn directly opposite the southernmost tip of Melville Island; the rest were inmates at the leper colony. The resulting total population of about 950, in 1954, is only about a hundred less than the figure of 1062 which Hart obtained in his census of 1928-29.

Marriage Arrangements

We have discussed how, under the traditional Tiwi pattern of life, the greatest energies of mature males were expended in bargaining with each other for new wives. The old social system was one which had as normal features prenatal and early childhood engagements for females, remarriage for all widows, considerable age difference between marriage partners, and polygamy. The new Catholic system introduced by Father Gsell outlawed, or at least discouraged, polygamous marriages, nuptial unions between persons of greatly differing ages, and all prenatal or childhood betrothals. As indicated, Father Gsell initiated his new policies by purchasing young females and then allowing them to choose their own partners from among their single agemates.

It is of interest to inspect the actual circumstances surrounding one of the earliest unions which took place under Father Gsell's supervision. About 1914, Polly, an attractive young female who had already had a rather checkered career, having been stolen by a Yuwatja male from her rightful mate, was "stolen back" by another Tiwi, Timalarua of the Rangwila. Polly, however, decided that she did not want an old husband like Timalarua, so she ran away to the sisters and Father Gsell. In time, old Timalarua allowed Father Gsell to buy this wife who did not want to live with him. Shortly afterward, Father Gsell asked Polly whom she wanted to marry. Polly named Cabbagee as the male of her choice and the couple soon set up housekeeping with Father Gsell's blessing. This was, at least, how the missionary saw it.

But what were the real circumstances surrounding this "free choice" by Polly? Her real father—that is, the husband to whom her mother Rita was married when Polly was born—had promised Polly to Kardu. Timalarua had "stolen" Polly from Kardu, her rightful husband. Nor is this the whole story. Rita had been "stolen" by Puti from Polly's father Turimpi. After several fights between Puti and the aging Turimpi and after Rita's complete refusal to return to Turimpi, Turimpi allowed Puti to keep Rita as his wife. Polly, however, was ultimately to go to the man to whom she had been promised, Kardu. But Puti, as the potential next father of Polly, had promised Cabbagee that as soon as Kardu died Polly was to be Cabbagee's wife. That is, when Polly chose Cabbagee as her mate she was only bypassing Kardu and taking as her husband the next normal alternative open to her.

When one considers what parts of Father Gsell's reform were significant in this case, one finds that only late consummation of marriage, monogamy, and marriage between agemates were important. A female did not actually have a "free choice" of her mate as Father Gsell had hoped and, in fact, had specified. She selected a youth to whom one of her relatives had at least tentatively promised her. Or (to put it in Hart's terms) she married—under Mission auspices—a young man who had at least a second or third mortgage on her.

Let us follow the case of Cabbagee's marriage further. He married Polly when he was about 23; he was too young to be married in the old pattern and was, therefore, happy to get a wife and be on his way up the social ladder. But when the next female promised to him (before her birth) came of age and he collected her, Polly made a terrific row. She did not want any younger female around her household as a second wife and told the priest at the Mission so. He in turn deprived Cabbagee of all gifts of tobacco and food and sent him and his family to the bush to think over the matter. After a few months, Cabbagee decided that he wanted tobacco and that after all the only place he could get it was at the Mission. He and his family returned and he gave up his second wife to Father Gsell, for a payment of food.

Younger men who were getting wives from among Father Gsell's convent girls thus found that they were unwise to accept a second wife from any other source. But such a young man, married under Catholic auspices, soon found that he could enhance his prestige without invoking criticism from the Mission if he gathered around him his own female relatives, the younger of whom he could give away later, one at a time, to men of his choice. A married man like Cabbagee, who gave another man his sister or sister's daughter, was in a position to ask all sorts of favors from the recipient, especially gifts of food, tobacco, and trade goods, and support in politics.

By the end of World War II, even these newer concepts of marriage agreement had begun to alter. There were many young Christian females desiring to have husbands whose fathers and brothers were not asking further wives as repayment. The fathers began to ask for new types of concessions from their future sons-in-law and demands which look very much like bride price and bride service developed as a basis for marriage arrangement. A young girl had a relatively "free choice" of her future spouse. But following this selection, her father let it be known to the young man what he expected. The desired payment was often stated in Australian money by the 1950's; some men were asking as much as a hundred pounds for a daughter. (This was a very high sum, since Tiwi males working for the Army received four pounds a week as normal wages.) Other men were asking that their sons-in-law live with them, thus leaving their own parental home, and contribute regularly to the upkeep of the household of the father-in-law. This was, indeed, quite a practical arrangement, for when such a young man went to work in Darwin his wife had to be supervised at home and, further, his employer was supposed to send home to the Mission part of the young man's wages.

Thus, by 1954, the following type of marriage agreement was initiated by the great majority of Tiwi with marriageable daughters, specifically those who centered their activities at Bathurst Island Mission and Garden Point. A young girl chose her future husband from her single, male agemates, sometimes with a suggestion from her father. Her father informed his future son-in-law of the obligations incumbent upon him, which normally included matrilocal postmarital residence and a bride price. An older woman with children, or even one without any offspring, who became a widow, was discouraged from remarrying by her father, if he survived, and by her brother after her father's death. The father or eldest brother of a widow with a daughter reaped the benefits of allowing that daughter to marry the young man whom she desired. The widow herself did not remarry but stayed in the household of her father or brother.

Residence Patterns

By 1953, traditional Tiwi residence patterns had undergone major modifications, some of which have already been mentioned. The old residence areas of the bands had been depopulated; in fact, nearly all the Tiwi were located around one of four European establishments—those at Darwin, Bathurst Island Mission, Garden Point, or Snake Bay. In each of these areas a centralized village pattern had developed. Within the Tiwi communities at Snake Bay, Garden Point, and Bathurst Island Mission there remained a few of the old large households with a polygamous base. But in all these camps the household heads were well past sixty and in most cases past seventy. Polygamous households were dying out by 1953.

But what was replacing them? One might assume that the European pattern of the single family household based upon neolocal residence would have emerged as the new Tiwi system. This was not the case, however. Just as Hart found in 1928-29 that successful Tiwi men were the heads of large establishments, so in 1953-54 the younger male leaders had gathered around them impressive collections of females. But these collections included now only one wife.

Let us consider again the case of Cabbagee. It will be remembered that his had been one of Father Gsell's first marriages and, except for a few uncomfortable months, he had been monogamous all his life. There were camped with him in 1954 a number of women and children who were related to him in many ways. There was his wife Polly, now a good Catholic who had taken the Christian name of Carmel, and her ancient mother Rita, who had borne a child long before the white man came to Bathurst Island. Also in "Cabbagee's camp," as the natives referred to it, was Patrick, Cabbagee's only son, and Patrick's wife. Patrick and his wife had three surviving children between the ages of four and thirteen; they also were raising 14-year-old Fabian, whose deceased father had been a "brother" of Patrick and whose deceased mother had been a "sister" of Patrick's wife. Cabbagee and Carmel (alias Polly) had three daughters, and Cabaggee had arranged with each son-in-law that he reside with Cabbagee and support him in his fights and politics. These daughters and sons-in-law had a total of ten children. The other members of Cabbagee's camp included the widow and children of Carmel's deceased younger maternal half-brother. Cabbagee had given this "sister" to Carmel's half-brother for his wife and when he died seven years later leaving a number of young children, Cabbagee defended the right of his "sister" not to remarry. With this "sister" of Cabbagee lived her step-mother and occasionally her real mother, until the latter died. Further, living in Cabbagee's camp were two of his full sister's daughters and their husbands, who became members of the camp by reason of the fact that Cabbagee arranged his sister's marriage in such a way that her husband, Babui, accepted Cabbagee as his leader.[1] When Babui arranged his own daughters' marriages, his new sons-in-law became subservient to Babui and thereby subservient to Cabbagee. Also resident in Cabbagee's camp at times were his younger paternal half-brother Pawpaw with his two surviving wives, his full brother Tommy's son, and two of their widowed "sisters" and their children.

We have mentioned here only that segment of Cabbagee's camp led by Cabbagee himself and that led by his half-brother Pawpaw, but such a listing is adequate for our purposes. It is noteworthy that the downward alteration in the age of marriage for males has meant that many less women become widows; first marriages of women last longer and, therefore, the system of patronage established at the time of the first marriage is more permanent. Babui's marriage, for example, had made him a henchman of Cabbagee from about 1920 to 1955. When women did become widows, especially if they had daughters, they were protected by their brothers who thereby became the "boss" of their daughters. The father or the "boss" of a girl arranged her mar-

---

[1] Hart would use the word "patron" in this relationship. Pilling prefers the word "leader." This is itself an indication of a certain subtle change in Tiwi social structure. The patron-satellite relationship of 1928-29 is nowadays better expressed as leader-follower. The pairs of men are closer in age than they used to be. How the Tiwi themselves now express the relationship is indicated in the next footnote.

riage with a boy who was willing to become the "worker" of the girl's controller.[2]

From the economic standpoint, the large household has much the same function as before the days of the Mission. The younger women go out together and gather food; the old women stay home with the young children. The younger men bring home choice items, which now are trade goods and money from Darwin. The "boss" of the great household is wealthy; today, he has food, tobacco, clothes, and usually sufficient money to gamble. The composition of the great households has altered, but their function is very much the same. The establishment of the monogamous Catholic Cabbagee is even larger than that of the polygamous old pagan, Ki-in-kumi, described in an earlier chapter; Cabbagee, with only one wife, has more women under his "control" than ever Ki-in-kumi had, despite his list of twenty-one wives. The Tiwi have thus been able to retain their large households even under the Mission-imposed system of monogamy.

The Change from Patriliny to Matriliny

In the pre-Cooper era of feuding, the largest significant units among the Tiwi were the bands; the Tiwi never, in that by-gone day, acted as a tribe, even in their attacks upon such outsiders as the British. In the 1950's, when informants talked of the old days they commonly mentioned that male members of old bands came together as units to go on war parties. These old bands did not have a strict rule of descent. But, as has already been indicated, the majority of the males were regarded all their lives as members of the band to which their father belonged. That is, the major unit of the old Tiwi social structure was patrilineal in emphasis.

There also existed in the old Tiwi pattern a strictly matrilineal clan organization, related primarily to totemism. One of the totemic animals of a clan stood for a member of that clan in the song composed to commemorate his death; for instance, the first line of the mourning song for a deceased male of the Red Paint Clan might be "I am red paint." Occasionally, several members of a clan helped one of their number in a fight, but this was apparently not very common before the Mission era. This clan-organization pattern prevailed among the Tiwi through about 1930. Then major and most unpredictable changes began.

What does one expect to happen when a society which has a patrilineal emphasis, like the old Tiwi one, comes into contact with a European society where, if there is any emphasis, it is a patrilineal one? Although one would ordinarily expect a strengthening of patriliny, such was not the case among the Tiwi. The old social unit which was predominantly patrilineal was a territorial group with its major functions in the system of feuding. When the

---

[2] By 1953, the terms "boss" and "worker" had come into the local Tiwi dialect to indicate superordinate and subordinate status interrelationships.

feuding system departed and the Tiwi community became more centralized, especially around the Bathurst Island Mission, the utility of the old band organization diminished and the underlying clan organization dominated. Suddenly, fighting was no longer in terms of band membership, for the matrilineal clan had become the only social unit of significance.

Today young Tiwi often deny that they have any band membership. But it is not unknown for teen-age Tiwi males to lie awake at night counting up the members of their matrilineal clan. According to informants, in the 1940's and 50's the major fights which occurred at Bathurst Island Mission were interclan skirmishes.

Thus, among the Tiwi, we have an example of how a society with a patrilineal emphasis under strong influence from another society with a patrilineal emphasis may, if there is an underlying matrilineal organization, become a society which is for all practical purposes solely matrilineal. The introductory student of anthropology is thereby warned that characterizations of societies as matrilineal or patrilineal are rarely adequate to form the basis for reconstructing past or predicting future forms of such societies.

Tiwi and the Australian Nation

Finally, let us consider those aspects of modern Tiwi life which attract national attention in Australia. What do the newspaper-reading members of the Australian public know about the Tiwi?

Probably the best known Tiwi is a male in his thirties, formerly known to other Tiwi and local residents of Darwin as Bobby Wilson. About 1953, an Australian movie producer, Charles Chauvel, went hunting for a "full-blood" aborigine who could act well enough to portray an aboriginal male in what became the Australian movie "Jedda." In Darwin, the producer found a football star from the Darwin group of Tiwi who could fill the part. Bobby Wilson soon was billed as Robert Tudawali.[3] He went "on location" at several spots in the Territory and finally traveled to Sydney for the studio shooting. The Sydney papers caught his story and spread his bearded face over the country. Bobby Wilson's photo from the local newspaper was hung up in several native huts at Bathurst Island Mission. After much publicity, he ultimately returned to his wife and their hut in the Bagot Native Compound in Darwin. Again the newshounds caught his story. According to them, he had returned to a life of degradation. The Australian public was shocked that a star of one of their best films should be discarded to live again like every other aborigine in Darwin. Tudawali was "rescued" and given a second role in another Australian film.

Bobby Wilson was only one of a large number of young Tiwi who are recognized as fine athletes. There are two football teams in Darwin which have Tiwi members: the Catholic team, St. Mary's, which often takes the local

---

[3] The last name Tudawali is an attempt to spell the Tiwi word for shark.

pennant, and the Wanderers, which draws from the permanent native population in Darwin and includes such Tiwi as Bobby Wilson. It is normal for one of these Tiwi players to be considered among the top three in Darwin football circles.

For a while, Edmund, a Tiwi from Bathurst Island Mission, was one of the players on the newly organized St. Mary's basketball team; other Tiwi have played on the Bagot Compound basketball team. Billy Larrakeyah, a Darwin Tiwi, was thought to have Olympic potentialities as a javelin thrower, but strained his arm in the try-outs.[4] Most recently, a group of young Catholic Tiwi has been organized into a water polo team called the Seals. National magazines suggest that they may be the best water polo team in the country, but so far they have not gone south to play any non-Darwin group.

Tiwi carving and painting have had recent popularity in Australian art circles. Traditional Tiwi graveposts are finely carved in geometric designs and painted with precise and complex networks of cross-hatching and other simple, but effective, motifs. The first modern innovation in Tiwi art occurred about 1945 when a native known as Katu (or Short Katu) made his first attempt to carve a human figure atop a mourning post. When Pilling later asked Katu why he had carved this post, he said, "Me see 'm along Darwin. Me savvy." That is, Katu transferred the concept of Western realistic statuary in the round into the Tiwi art form. He carved a second realistic post for presentation to Queen Elizabeth II in 1954. More recently, Tiwi carvers at Snake Bay have taken to realistic carving. Two figurines, both carved by Tiwi at Snake Bay, were given to the Perth Museum in 1958. Sixteen mourning posts from Snake Bay were purchased by the National Art Gallery in Sydney the same year. An art display of Tiwi carving has been held in the United States in Philadelphia.

Tiwi have received recognition in the Northern Territory for other art forms. One of the thirty-year-old female Tiwi at Bathurst Island Mission usually takes first prize for embroidery at the annual Territorial fair. There has also been interest shown by outsiders in the double-barbed ceremonial spears. Male Tiwi skill in dancing has attracted wide attention in Australia. When natives from all over the Territory were sent to dance before Queen Elizabeth in Queensland during her 1954 tour, three Tiwi were among the delegation. The Tiwi contingent, directed by the innovator Short Katu, made every news story covering this part of the Royal Visit. In Darwin, when Bagot Compound needs to raise money for native participation in sports, the Tiwi, usually led by Katu, present a public dance. As a result, Katu's clan under his direction has invented many new dances for white Australian audiences.

Perhaps we may look forward to the day when American television audiences can enjoy such a Tiwi dance, one of Australia's best native products. Yet only sixty years ago, and therefore in the lifetime of many people still living, very few Tiwi had even seen a white man, and white men who set foot on Tiwi soil, like Cooper in his first attempt in 1897, were ferociously chased out.

---

[4] He was killed in a brawl in Darwin in the spring of 1959.

References Cited

Historical References

CONIGRAVE, C. PRICE, 1936, *North Australia*. London: Jonathan Cape.

EARL, GEORGE WINDSOR, 1853, *The Native Races of the Indian Archipelago*: *Papuans*. London: Hippolyte Bailliere.

HEERES, J. E., 1899, *The Part Borne by the Dutch in the Discovery of Australia 1606-1765*. London: Luzac & Company.

MANDER JONES, PHYLLIS, 1948, *The Tasman Map of 1644*. Sydney: The Trustees of the Public Library of New South Wales.

TINDALE, NORMAN, 1956, The Peopling of Southeastern Australia. *Australian Museum Magazine*, Vol. XII, No. 4.

Anthropological References

BERNDT, R. M., 1955, "Murngin" (Wulamba) social organization. *American Anthropologist*, 57: 84-106.

———, 1957, In Reply to Radcliffe-Brown on Australian Local Organization. *American Anthropologist*, 59: 346-351.

ELKIN, A. P., and R. M. and C. H. BERNDT, 1951, Social Organization of Arnhem Land. *Oceania XXX*, No. 4, 253-301.

HART, C. W. M., 1930, The Tiwi of Melville and Bathurst Islands. *Oceania I*, 167-180.

———, 1931, Personal Names among the Tiwi. *Oceania I*, 280-290.

———, 1954, The Sons of Turimpi. *American Anthropologist*, 56: 242-261.

———, 1955, Contrasts between Prepubertal and Postpubertal Education. In

Education and Anthropology, G. D. Spindler (ed.). Stanford, Calif.: Stanford University Press.

MOUNTFORD, CHARLES P., 1958, *The Tiwi, Their Art, Myth and Ceremony.* London: Phoenix House.

MURDOCK, GEORGE PETER, 1949, *Social Structure.* New York: Macmillan.

RADCLIFFE-BROWN, A. R., 1912, Three Tribes of Western Australia. *J. A. I.,* XLIII, 143-194.

————, 1930, Former Numbers and Distribution of the Australian Aborigines. In *Official Year Book of the Commonwealth of Australia,* No. 23.

————, 1930-31, The Social Organization of Australian Tribes. Oceania Monographs No. 1. *Oceania I,* Nos. 1-4.

————, 1956, On Australian Local Organization. *American Anthropologist,* 58: 363-367.

SHARP, ANDREW, 1957, *Ancient Voyagers in the Pacific.* London: Penguin Books.

SPENCER, BALDWIN, 1914, *The Native Tribes of the Northern Territory of Australia.* London: Macmillan.

WARNER, W. LLOYD, 1937, *A Black Civilization.* New York: Harper.

Recommended Reading

Australia and Adjacent Areas

The Pacific

OLIVER, DOUGLAS L., 1951, *The Pacific Islands*. Cambridge, Mass.: Harvard University Press.

GARDINER, LYNDSAY, 1957, *Pacific Peoples*. London, Melbourne, New York: Longmans, Green.

The Australian Aborigines

BERNDT, R. M. and C. H., 1952, *The First Australians*. Sydney: Ure Smith.

A short, simple, and very sound attempt to summarize the life of the aborigines for the general reader. Written by two professional anthropologists (a husband and wife team) with extensive fieldwork experience in Arnhem Land.

DARK, ELEANOR, 1941, *The Timeless Land*. New York: Macmillan.

Written in novel form but draws heavily upon documentary sources, both of history and anthropology. Concerned with the impact of the early white settlers upon the culture of the aborigines.

HART, C. W. M., 1954, The Sons of Turimpi. *American Anthropologist*, Vol. 56, 242-261.

Brief article that uses five Tiwi brothers to show that "personalities" in simple cultures differ as much as among ourselves and therefore disputes the theory that people in simple cultures are standardized.

MOUNTFORD, CHARLES P., 1948, *Brown Men and Red Sand*. Melbourne: Robertson and Mullens.

The author has traveled extensively in the most barren and isolated areas of Central Australia and therefore among the most isolated and primitive surviving tribesmen. Excellent pictures of native life in the deserts.

SIMPSON, COLIN, 1952, *Adam in Ochre*. Sydney: Angus and Robertson, New York: Anglobooks.

By an Australian newspaperman who writes in very superior journalistic style about the "primitive areas" of the Pacific. Very informative and up-to-date. (The same author has two other books, *Adam with Arrows* (1954) and *Adam in Plumes* (1955), describing the natives of New Guinea.)

SPENCER, BALDWIN, and F. J. GILLEN, 1927, *The Arunta* (2 vols.). London: Macmillan.

Usually regarded as an anthropological classic. Deals with the Arunta as they were about 1910. Written by a professor of zoology, who visited, and a policeman, who lived with, the Arunta. Gives much space to ceremonials and little to interpersonal relations and everyday life.

WARNER, W. LLOYD, 1937, *A Black Civilization*. New York: Harper.

Very good account of the Murngin of eastern Arnhem Land. Much more modern than Spencer and Gillen and strong at the points where they are weak. The author later used the same fieldwork methods to study Yankee City in New England.